Crappie: How to Catch Them Spring and Summer

Copyright © 2012 , John E. Phillips

Table of Contents

Chapter 1 - What Are the Myths about the Crappie Spawn

Editor's Note: Ronnie Capps and his partner, Steve Coleman, of Tiptonville, Tennessee, have won numerous World-Champion crappie tournaments and have earned over $1.5-million catching crappie. "But I think we've spent all that money entering and traveling to crappie tournaments," Capps says with a smile.

In this chapter, Ronnie Capps explains when the crappie spawn starts, where to find the fish during the spawn and how to catch crappie when a cold front hits. He'll dispel crappie myths most of us embrace as fact. Most of us believe the best time to catch crappie, if not the only time, is when the crappie are spawning and holding on shallow-water cover. But do the crappie always spawn in shallow-water

1

cover? And, where do crappie spawn when there's little or no shallow-water cover?

What about the Crappie Spawn

Question: Ronnie, what water temperatures and weather conditions cause crappie to spawn?

Capps: When the water temperature hits 59 degrees, then you need to start looking for the white crappie to begin their spawn. If an area has rising water and a temperature of 59 to 60 degrees, that's when the crappie will move into the more shallow water to spawn. The black crappie probably will have spawned-out by this time.

Question: When do the black crappie start to spawn?

Capps: Of course, the black-crappie spawn is at different times in various places, but the Reelfoot Lake crappie tournament near our home always is held during the first week of March. The females generally will be were spawning and have eggs running off their tails then. What's amazing is during this tournament we fished on Reelfoot Lake and found crappie spawning during was exactly 7 days after ice melted from the lake. Seven days before the tournament, the air temperature was 14 degrees with ice covering parts of the lake. However, a week later the surface temperature was about 60 degrees, and the water temperature was close to 56 degrees. I've always found that black crappie usually spawn before the white crappie do. The spawn usually is over for black crappie by the third week in March in our section of north Tennessee.

Question: So, Ronnie, we're looking for 59-degree water. Once we find that water temperature, on what types of places will the crappie be holding?

Capps: The male crappie will be the first ones you start catching, especially on lakes that are heavily stained. If you're fishing lakes where the water level fluctuates quite a bit, like Grenada Lake in Mississippi, those crappie will move in as close to the bank as they can get, while still being in the water. But in a reservoir like Reelfoot Lake in Tennessee, where the water level remains stable, the male crappie won't go to the bank. I have a friend who fishes Grenada, and when the water starts rising, he says that every day he'll fish more shallow than the previous day. He's told me that he goes and looks at a tree top on dry ground, and the following day he returns to that same treetop, and the water will have risen, and then he'll catch crappie there. So that's how fast male crappie can move on lakes where the water level rises in the spring.

My theory is if you're wade fishing for crappie on one of these types of lakes, you don't want to fish any deeper than your butt cheeks, and preferably fish shallower than that. Male crappie usually will be caught in 2-1/2- to-3 feet of water on a lake with rising water. In other words, 59 degrees on a lake with rising water means to fish today where you've walked yesterday. If you're fishing from a boat, then the back ends of coves, pockets and bays often will heat-up between 65 and 67 degrees on really-bright, warm and sunny days, when the water temperature on the main lake may only be 59 degrees.

Question: Okay, Ronnie, where are you going to locate crappie during the spawn on lakes that are stable, where the water temperature doesn't fluctuate like at Reelfoot Lake in Tennessee?

Capps: The crappie at Reelfoot will move vertically on the structure that's available to them, instead of going to the shore. For instance, there may be cut-off stumps that come-up from the bottom at 12 feet. But the crappie may be spawning on tops of those stumps in 2 foot of water. So, on stable lakes, instead of moving to the bank, the male crappie move-up in the water column to find structure where the females can spawn. Sometimes they will move-up a little shallower, but they'll still be spawning on logs and stumps in 2 feet of water.

Question: What about the crappie spawn in deep and clear lakes, like Smith Lake in north Alabama, which is one of the deepest and clearest lakes in the state?

Capps: You may find male and female fish spawning as deep as 25 feet in deep, clear lakes. I have caught male fish that still have had color in them spawning in 25 feet of water on the tops of stumps, during the month of June, in Cedars Creek, Ohio. So in deep, clear lakes, the crappie often will spawn later and deeper than they do in lakes where the water rises in the spring. Even on Kentucky Lake, you'll often find male fish moving in to prepare a nest on top of stumps in 10 to 17 feet of water. Therefore, remember that not all crappie move into shallow water close to the bank during the spawn. The type of lake, the depth of the water and the clarity of the water all affect when and where the crappie will spawn.

How Long a Crappie Spawn Lasts

Question: Ronnie, how long does the crappie spawn last?

Capps: Most people believe the crappie spawn only lasts for about 2 weeks, but I've found that the crappie spawn can last into the summer. Remember that the crappie spawn doesn't happen all at once. Although there's definitely a peak of the spawn, some crappie lag behind and don't spawn until the summer. I've seen male crappie stay on a bed well into June in some areas. The female crappie lays her eggs within a matter of hours, but then the male crappie hangs around the bed, guarding the fry. I've seen male crappie go on the nest in March and still be on the nest in June, with the females coming in and out of the nest during this time. When the males are guarding the nest, they want to kill or run off bait rather than try to eat it. I've never caught a big male with his belly full of shad or baitfish. Generally a male crappie will have an empty stomach in May and often into June.

However, a female loaded-up with eggs, usually will have a lot of shad in her belly and be loaded-up on food. While that female is carrying eggs, she's eating everything in sight. After she spawns, she's slow to recover. There's usually a 2-week period or longer when the female doesn't eat much. She's kind of like an old hound dog that's just given birth to pups. She looks pretty rough the first 2 weeks to a month after giving birth, but then she starts to eat again, fatten-up and look healthy.

At Kentucky Lake, by mid-June, I can catch some female crappie pretty deep, and they'll be filled-out and recovered from the spawn. I'll catch these female crappie in 18 to 20 feet of water on the same structure where I've caught them earlier in the year before the spawn's started. I have a little place I fish on Kentucky Lake before the water temperature hits 59 degrees, and I can catch crappie anytime I fish there. The deepest part of the basin is about 30-foot deep, and the rim of the basin is about 20-foot deep. During the pre-spawn, the crappie always are holding there. But after the spawn, I can return to that same basin and catch crappie from the end of May into the beginning of June.

So, many times the spawn lasts much longer than most people think. If you understand the spawn, you'll know where to catch the crappie before the water temperature reaches 59 degrees, signaling the spawn, as well as where to catch crappie after the spawn has occurred. You can catch crappie not only during the spawn, but also during the pre-spawn and the post-spawn.

Chapter 2 - How to Find and Catch March Crappie

Finding Early-Spring Crappie in Kentucky with Malcolm Lane

Editor's Note: Malcolm Lane of Kuttawa, Kentucky, guides on Lake Barkley and Kentucky Lake for both crappie and bass and also catches sauger in March. Because Lane's on the water every day and has to produce crappie, bass and sauger for his clients, we've asked him how to find and catch fish at this time of year.

Question: How do you catch crappie in March?

Lane: I catch most of my crappie vertical jigging with hair jigs and plastic jigs tipped with minnows. I prefer to fish with 1/8-ounce Mister Twister Lightnin' Bugs because they have a little mylar in them, which gives them a little flash. When the water's really cold, I like to fish hair jigs tipped with minnows about half the time, because bigger crappie are caught with a minnow on the jig.

Question: What color jig do you use?

Lane: I like chartreuse-and-black, but if the water clears up, I prefer pink or blue. I'm generally fishing these jigs on 4- or 6-pound-test line with a 9-1/2-foot fly rod.

Question: Around what kind of structure do you fish?

Lane: In March, I fish around brush piles on creek channels. I also fish Porcupine trees (PVC pipes that come together in a hub and spoke out from that hub) out in 10 to 25 feet of water. Our lakes are getting a little bit older now, and the bottoms are becoming cleaner. So, anglers are putting out hickory trees and Porcupine Fish Attractors

9

to help rebuild structure in the lake. If the crappie are aggressive in the early spring, they'll either be holding above or at the edge of the brush. But if they're not aggressive, they'll be holding down in the brush. You'll have to thread your jig through the brush to reach them. When this section of Kentucky is hit by a cold front, the crappie don't want to bite. That's when you've got to fish the Lightnin' Bug jig down in the brush. Using 6-pound-test line, you often can straighten the hook on that jig. But even if you don't straighten the hook, the line will break, and you won't tear up the brush.

Question: Malcolm, what's another tactic you use to catch crappie in March?

Lane: In March, the crappie are either extremely deep or shallow. If they're shallow, I'm still fishing a Lightnin' Bug jig, but I'm fishing a smaller size under a bobber tipped with a minnow. If the water's cold, I'll attract more strikes by tipping the bait with a minnow than if I don't tip the bait with a minnow. If the water's a little dingy, and the area gets some sunshine, the warmest water will be right up against the shoreline. So, I'll set my bobber to suspend the Mister Twister Lightnin' Bug jig about 2- to 3-feet deep. I'll cast the jig to the shoreline and work that jig under the bobber. You can move the bait really slowly, or you can twitch it. I'm more of a twitcher. I get more strikes twitching the jig than when I reel it slowly. I prefer the 1/32-ounce jig when I'm fishing shallow water. I like to swim the light jig over shoreline brush and then stop the jig and let it fall on the other side of the brush. If I twitch the jig, I can twitch it over cover and stop it on the other side of the cover. At this time of year, I'm catching crappie that weigh from 1-3/4- to 2-pounds each. To catch a 2-pound-or-more crappie, I wait until later in the year when the female crappie is full of eggs.

Question: How many crappie do you catch in a day?

Lane: If I'm fishing when there's a bad cold front, I may only catch two or three crappie in a day. But if a warm front comes into the area, or the water's stable, I generally can catch 20 or more crappie in a day. The legal limit in Kentucky is 20 crappie per person at the first of March.

Question: Malcolm, what other lure do you fish for March crappie?

Lane: Many times I'll fish a 1/16-ounce jig on 6-pound-test line with a 2-inch Curly Tail Grub and catch crappie all day. I fish a lot of chartreuse, black and even yellow. White is still productive in March. If I only can choose one color to fish, it probably will be chartreuse because it seems to be the best color all day, every day.

Question: How do you fish the Curly Tails?

Lane: I fish the Curly Tail Grubs with a slow retrieve, casting them to the shore and then creepy-crawling them out to deep water. If you don't know what to do when you're crappie fishing, put a 1/16-ounce Curly Tail Grub on 6-pound-test line, cast it out toward the shoreline, reel it in, and you'll catch crappie. I'll fish line as light as 4-pound test, using jigs as light as 1/32-ounce. I generally keep several-different colors of grubs. So, regardless of the water condition, I can match the color of jig to the color of water I fish. If you've got the Twister Tail grubs and the Lightnin' Bug jigs, you're prepared to catch crappie in almost any crappie-fishing situation. I catch numbers of crappie at Lake Barkley and Kentucky Lake, and I depend on these jigs to produce crappie for me and my customers.

Minnesota Crappie through the Ice in March with Matt Johnson

Editor's Note: Matt Johnson, from Blaine, Minnesota, fishes southern Minnesota and the Horseshoe Chain of lakes and often guides as many as 6 days a week for both ice fishing and open-water fishing. Although he'll guide for any of the species found in Minnesota, he's a panfish specialist.

Question: How are you catching most of your crappie?

Johnson: I like to fish with plastic lures and rarely use live bait when I go fishing, except when I'm converting a live-bait fisherman to being a plastic-bait fisherman. I only carry minnows, maggots and worms to teach people how to fish plastic baits. But I'll explain that later. My favorite baits for panfish are the Mister Twister Micro Shad, Micro Nymph and Micro Crawfish, because I try to imitate exactly on what the bluegills and the crappie are feeding. When I fish with these small soft plastics, I'll often use some type of float. Then I can cast the bait to the fish's strike zone and let the bait sit in the strike zone for a longer time than if I'm casting and retrieving. A float allows me to keep my bait at the depth where I think the fish are feeding. Also floats make my casting easier. I can cast further and stay further away from the fish, so that I don't spook them. I jig with plastics in deep water, and I fish with floats in shallow water.

Question: Matt, are you fishing deep water or shallow water in late February and March?

Johnson: Right now we're fishing on the ice and not fishing from boats at all. So, when I'm fishing through the ice, I fish all different depths. If the water gets a lot of oxygen in it and still has green weeds, I'll fish shallow. But if there's not a lot of oxygen in the water, I'll fish deep.

Question: Okay, how do you rig for crappie and bluegills at this time of year?

Johnson: When I'm ice fishing, I'm using a horizontal presentation. I like a jig that doesn't have a collar. I like to thread the Micro Shad, onto the jig, so that the plastic is straight to make it look natural. I like the 1-1/8-inch Micro Shad because it presents a small profile and exactly imitates what we call pin minnows that we find in our waters. We call these fish pin minnows because they're so tiny. Often the crappie will herd these pin minnows into the shallow weeds and gorge themselves on these pin minnows as they feed along the edges of the weeds.

Question: Matt, how do you find the places where you're going to fish?

Johnson: I use a Marcum Flasher depth finder, which is very similar to a Vexilar flasher. This flasher is round, features three different colors and is so sensitive that it not only shows the bottom and the fish but also my Micro Shad jig. Too, I can detect weeds and tell whether the bottom is soft or hard with this depth finder. If the ice is thin and clear, especially in the early part of the season, you can slide the transducer over the ice and locate the weed edges and the fish. However, at this time of the year, with a foot of snow cover over the ice, I have to punch holes in the ice when I'm looking for fish. I use a hand-held Lowrance depth finder to help me locate the spots on the lakes where I want to fish. I put the map chips of the lake in this depth finder to enable me to see the contours of the lake, which cuts-down on the amount of time I have to spend looking for drop-offs and weed lines. If I can find green weeds under the ice, then I look for the first bottom break in 7 to 12 feet of water. If I can't locate those bottom breaks, I look for structure on the edges of deep holes out in the lake.

Most fishermen will be searching for that structure on the edges of those deep holes. So, the fish staying in those areas receive the most fishing pressure. That's why I really prefer to identify secondary drop-offs away from those deep holes. Once I identidy the location I want to fish, I drill my holes in the ice, put my depth finder over the hole and then drop my Micro Shad down in the water to the depth where I see the fish holding.

Question: What size jig head are you using on that Micro Shad?

Johnson: I don't use any jig head that's heavier than 1/16-ounce. Generally, I use a 1/32- or a 1/64-ounce jig head – really-small profile baits. We generally fish very-small jigs during the wintertime.

Question: What color Micro Shad are you using for March crappie through the ice?

Johnson: My two personal favorites are pearl-white and pearl-pink. And I'm fishing them on 3-pound-test made by P-Line. The line, called Fluroclear is a copolymer, a monofilament coated with fluorocarbon. The advantages to this type of line are that it has very-little memory to it, it's invisible, it has tremendous knot strength, and it helps shed water, which helps with freeze-up. I can watch the jig fall from the surface down to the depth where I see the fish images on my depth finder. I feel like I'm looking at an adult video game, because the fish show up in different colors, depending on what size they are. The sonar picks up the air bladders of the fish. When the jig image is overlapped by the fish image, I can set the hook, whether I feel the bite or not.

However, I still use spring bobbers attached to my rod, because the spring bobber either rises or falls when a crappie bites. Particularly during the winter months, we catch a lot of up-biting fish. When the fish are biting-up you may not notice the strike, if you don't have a spring bobber. When the fish picks up your bait, if it's biting up, the spring will lift up. And you won't be able to feel that light bite through the rod without a spring bobber.

Question: How deep is the water you're fishing now during the first part of March?

Johnson: I'm fishing 16- to 20-feet deep. And, we catch both crappie and bluegills at that depth. Oftentimes during the winter, the crappie and bluegills will school together, which will allow you to catch both fish out of the same ice hole.

South Carolina and North Carolina March Crappie with Stokes McClellan

Editor's Note: Stokes McClellan from Huntersville, North Carolina, is a tournament crappie fisherman and a crappie-fishing enthusiast.

Question: Stokes, where do you fish for March crappie, and how are you catching them?

16

McClellan: I fish Clarks Hill, Lake Wylie and Lake Jordan.

Question: How will you catch crappie during March?

McClellan: Right now, the crappie are staging for the spawn in the mouths of the creeks and the bays. I'm finding crappie from the mouths of the creeks and the bays to about 1/4 the length of that creek or bay. The crappie seem to be holding 14- to 16-feet deep, suspended above deeper water. If we have a couple of consecutively warm days, the crappie will move-up in the water column about 6 feet below the surface. Even though the crappie are bunched-up, there are still quite a few scattered fish. So, I'll long -line troll for them. Our water temperature is 49 to 50 degrees in March. When the water temperature rises a few degrees, the crappie will move-up onto the banks to start spawning.

Question: Which poles are you using for longlining?

McClellan: I like the B 'n' M Pro Staff poles and the Sam Heaton Super-Sensitive poles. I'll use the B 'n' M Pro Staff poles in lengths ranging from 10 to 16 feet. In the Sam Heaton Super-Sensitive pole, I like the 9-foot poles.

Question: How are you long-line trolling?

McClellan: I have my poles in pole holders on the back of my boat. I'll put my 16-foot poles straight off the side of the boat, so they can reach out further on either side of the boat than my other poles.

Question: Why are you putting your poles out of the back of your boat instead of the front like most crappie fishermen who long-line troll?

McClellan: The back of my boat is 7-feet wide, and by having two 16-foot B 'n' M poles on either side of my boat, I can troll about 39 feet of water when I make a pass with my boat. By trolling from the back of the boat, when I do get a crappie on one of my lines, the crappie I'm catching doesn't tangle-up the other lines quite as much as the fish will when I'm trolling out of the front of the boat. I'm sitting down in the boat while I'm trolling.

Question: How are you running your trolling motor on the front of the boat when you're sitting on the back of the boat?

McClellan: I use a Minn Kota AutoPilot trolling motor. I've got a controller that plugs into the trolling motor with 18 feet of cable that allows me to sit in the back of the boat and direct the trolling motor, which is on the front of the boat.

Question: What size jigs are you using?

McClellan: I'm trolling 1/8-ounce jigs. But if we have those warming days, and the crappie move up to 6 feet of water I'll start pulling 1/16-ounce jigs. In late March when the crappie move higher in the water column, I'll pull 1/32-ounce jigs. When the water temperature hits 52 or 53 degrees, the crappie will move up to 3- and 4-foot water depths, so I'll need a lighter jig to pull through more-shallow water.

Question: How far behind the boat are you trolling?

McClellan: I usually troll 75- to 90-feet behind the boat.

Question: How did you decide to troll that far behind the boat?

McClellan: I let the lines in the center of the boat out to about 90-feet behind the boat because the boat may spook some of the crappie holding in 6 feet of water. So I want the center lines to be further behind the boat. Then if the boat does spook the fish as I pass over them, my jigs will run a little deeper and be in front of those the fish than the lines on the sides of my boat. The lines on the 16-foot poles will run about 75-feet behind the boat, since the crappie that are further away won't be as spooked as much by the boat's movement as the crappie directly under the boat. When the crappie move up shallow, and I start fishing 1/32-ounce jigs, most of the crappie I catch will be on the rods furthest away from the boat.

Question: What pound-test line are you using?

McClellan: I fish exclusively with 4-pound-test line, because I've found it's much-less visible to the fish than 6-pound-test line is. Because I've fished 4-pound test line for many years, I can better determine what depth my jigs are running at when I'm fishing 4-pound test. If I change to 6-pound-test line, the depths at which my jigs are running may change by as much as 2 feet.

Question: What color jigs do you like at this time of year?

McClellan: In dingy, off-color or muddy water, I like oranges, browns, blacks and blues. I'll stick with the darker colors on overcast days as well. In clear water, I like chartreuse, bubblegum pink or white.

Question: In a day of fishing, how many crappie do you expect to catch?

McClellan: On a good day in March, my catching 50 to 75 crappie isn't uncommon. The last trip I went on, my two biggest fish weighed 2.59 pounds and 2.6 pounds. When we start catching the big females, they'll usually weigh from 1-1/2 to 2-1/2-pounds each.

Tunica Cut-Off During March and April with Ed "Dawg" Weldon

Editor's Note: Ed "Dawg" Weldon of Tunica, Mississippi, has fished the Tunica Cut-Off, a large oxbow lake off the Mississippi River in Tunica, Mississippi, for more than 60 years. Like most oxbows, the Tunica Cut-Off is affected by rising and falling river levels, as well as temperature changes.

Question: Dawg, in late March and April, where do you find crappie at the Tunica Cut-Off?

Weldon: The crappie are moving toward the shallow banks, and at this time of year, they either will be preparing to spawn, spawning or just finished spawning. The crappie really like three things – rising water levels, which inundate new bushes, trees and grass; warm-water temperatures, which you generally will find in shallow oxbow lakes like the Tunica Cut-Off that warm-up quicker and stay warmer longer than the water in the Mississippi River; and areas where there's no wind. One other factor that seems to influence the crappie and where to find them is the amount of new water created when the river level rises, and the water in the Tunica Cut-Off begins to back-up. All these elements come together during the period from mid-March to mid-April here at Tunica.

Question: At what depth will you find the crappie?

Weldon: The crappie generally will be in water from 1-1/2- to 3-feet deep. I've fished here my entire life, and the crappie always show-up in places where they historically have gone at this time of year. So, I usually know where to locate crappie every year.

Question: Around what type of structure do you fish?

Weldon: I prefer to fish the little stick-ups, many of which are isolated, that you can see when the water rises. Usually these stick-ups are the top parts of a small bush or branch, and the rest of the limbs and the body of the tree will be underwater, providing plenty of cover for the pre-spawn or the spawning crappie.

Question: What jig, pole and line do you use to catch these shallow-water crappie?

Weldon: I use a 1/32-ounce jig with 12-pound-test Gold Stren line on a pole.

Question: Why do you use 12-pound-test line when most crappie fishermen fish with 6- to 4-pound-test line?

Weldon: At this time of year, we generally catch really-big crappie weighing from 1-1/2- to 2-pounds each. Occasionally, we'll get a really-nice-sized bass on the line, so I want a line strong enough to hold a big crappie or bass that takes the jig and heads for thick cover. Too, I want a line strong enough that if I have to get a big fish in the boat quickly and don't have a dip net, the line won't break when I bring that slab over the side of my boat. Since I'm tight-line fishing, I prefer the gold-colored. I can see the bite better than on clear-colored line or other line colors. Now, I can't tell if the big, gold-colored line makes any difference in the number of crappie I catch.

Question: What color jig do you like at this time of year?

Weldon: I prefer a black-head jig with either a chartreuse or a yellow body skirt.

Question: What pole do you use?

Weldon: I like the 10-foot B'n'M Buck's Ultimate Pole. I fish to catch crappie, not play with crappie. So, when I get a bite, I want a pole strong enough to jack a 2- to a 3-pound crappie out of the water and bring it to the boat, without the crappie getting hung-up in the brush or around a stump. This pole has the strength, power and the hook-setting ability I need. Then when I set the hook on the crappie, as soon as the crappie feels the hook, the crappie's head is coming out of the water and is airborne before it realizes it's hooked.

Question: In a day of fishing the Tunica Cut-Off in March and April, how many crappie do the people fishing with you generally catch, and what size are they?

Weldon: We usually catch about 20 or 30 crappie per person, weighing from 1-1/2- to 2-pounds-plus each.

Question: What makes the Tunica Cut-Off such a great place to catch crappie at this time of year?

Weldon: When the Mississippi River begins to rise, and the crappie come out of the river and the deep holes looking for warmer water temperatures, freshly-inundated land and warm, sunny banks where they can spawn, the crappie just have to come to the Tunica Cut-Off. The Cut-Off has plenty of baitfish, ideal habitat, shallow water, warm-water temperatures and brushy places where the crappie can spawn. There's nothing else these crappie can want that they won't find in the Cut-Off. Too, the Cut-Off has deep holes, so if we get one of those freaky cold fronts that run the crappie off the bank, the crappie don't have to travel far to get into a deep hole and stay close to the spawning grounds.

Question: How do you catch those crappie when your area gets those cold fronts or a dramatic weather change?

Weldon: When the crappie bite gets finicky at this time of year, I put Berkley PowerBait Crappie Nibbles on the backs of my jigs. Anytime I know where the crappie are holding, but I'm not catching them with a straight jig, I'll use the Crappie Nibbles.

Question: What part of the lake is the best spot to find crappie right now?

Weldon: Generally the first place where the crappie start showing-up is in the upper end of the lake where the water's usually warmer, and there's less wind.

Black Crappie on Reelfoot Lake in March with Billy Blakely

Editor's Note: Billy Blakely, chief hunting and fishing guide at Blue Bank Resort near Tiptonville, Tennessee, has guided and fished on Reelfoot Lake for over 20 years. From first light until dark, more than 300 days a year, Blakely is fishing for crappie or bass.

Question: Billy, how are you finding and catching crappie in March at Reelfoot?

Blakely: We're catching two-different kinds of crappie in various ways. We're catching black crappie in shallow water and white crappie in deep water.

Question: How are you catching black crappie, Billy?

Blakely: We're fishing a cork and a jig on a crappie pole in about 2 feet of water around the lily pads.

Question: How you are rigging for the crappie?

Blakely: I'm using 4-pound-test line and a small slip bobber up the line with a 1/16-ounce black-and-chartreuse jig tied on the end of the line to have enough weight on the line of my pole to cast it. The lilies are still about 12- to 14-inches underwater. The black crappie relate to shallow water year-round on Reelfoot. They've been there all year feeding on shad. By rigging like this, your jig stays above the underwater lily pad, and a crappie will come up out of those stems to get your jig. We're catching some really-nice-sized crappie right now, weighing up to 2-1/4-pounds each.

Question: Billy, how concentrated are these crappie?

Blakely: If you fish 100 yards of lily pads, you may fish with your pole for 80 yards and only catch three or four crappie. But then in that last 20 yards, you may catch 40 to 60 crappie. The good news is once you find the crappie, you generally can return to the same spot for 3 or 4 days and continue to catch crappie.

Question: Billy, how are you reaching those shallow-water black crappie?

Blakely: We pull the motor all the way up out of the water and use an electric anchor on the front of the boat and the back of the boat. Then we can ease the anchor down into the water without spooking the fish. The secret to catching black crappie at Reelfoot is to be extremely quiet on the shallow water. If you make noise, you won't catch the black crappie. That's why I've put carpet in the bottom of my boat to help muffle the noise. Remember, our boat is only in 18 to 20 inches of water, so we need a shallow-draft boat to reach these areas.

The White Crappie Are Deep on Reelfoot Lake in March with Billy Blakely

Question: Billy, you've explained that the black crappie on Reelfoot in March, are holding in about 8 inches of water over a 2-foot bottom. Where are you finding the white crappie in March?

Blakely: We're fishing 18-feet deep in 20 feet of water when we're fishing for white crappie. We'll be spider rigging (slow-trolling) with our poles when we're fishing for those deep-water white crappie. With the cool weather our area's having in March, the white crappie will be holding right on the bottom. When we're fishing for white crappie, we're fishing minnows only, hooking the minnows in the eyes with a double-hook rig so they appear to be swimming. That 20-foot-deep water has stumps on its bottom, so we're trolling just above the stumps. Reelfoot Lake is a really-shallow lake, and there's not much 20-foot water in this lake.

Question: In one day of fishing for white crappie, how many will you and your customers usually catch in March?

Blakely: We'll generally catch 40 to 80 white crappie on a good day that will weigh from 3/4- to about 3-pounds each.

Question: Billy, last week you mentioned that black crappie concentrate in about 18 inches of water, and now you're saying white crappie hold in about 18 feet of water. How do you decide when you go fishing which kind of crappie you'll target?

Blakely: We let the weather decide for us.

Question: Under what conditions do you fish for each type of crappie?

Blakely: When we're fishing for black crappie, we prefer windy and cloudy weather conditions. On windy and cloudy days, we use our boat to quietly move into that shallow water without the crappie being able to see us or hear us very well. When Reelfoot Lake has clear days and not much wind, we'll sit on the front end of our boat and spider rig for white crappie in deep water. We can fish successfully in 15- to 20-mile-per-hour winds. However, when we get a wind that creates white caps on the lake, we move into the backwater and the shallow areas and fish for black crappie. So, we let the weather conditions dictate what type of crappie we're targeting. On rough days, we go to the shallow water for black crappie. On calm days, we fish the deep water for white crappie.

Question: Billy, why don't you fish the lily pads in shallow water on clear days?

Blakely: The crappie are just like bass in clear, calm water. They can see and hear you better on clear days in the shallow water. Now, you may catch a few, but you won't catch nearly as many crappie as you will if you fish the deeper water for the white crappie.

Chapter 3 - How to Catch Crappie in March and April with Billy Blakely

Editor's Note: Reelfoot Lake in the northwestern corner of Tennessee, near Hornbeak, Tennessee, about 2-miles from the Mississippi River, is one of the most-productive crappie-fishing lakes in the nation. Anglers catch crappie there year-round in large numbers. At one time not too-many years ago, so many crappie were in the lake that they were caught and sold commercially. However, today there's no commercial crappie fishing at Reelfoot, but anglers come from all over the country to fish its waters. Some of the best crappie-tournament fishermen anywhere also live on the banks of Reelfoot. This past week I fished with Billy Blakely, the chief guide for Blue Bank Resort on Reelfoot Lake. The weather was terrible. The wind was blowing, the waves were slapping the boat, but we still caught fish.

During March and April, Reelfoot Lake is loaded with
crappie fishermen, and not without good reason. The lake's
bottom is covered with fallen trees, stumps and logs.
Reelfoot is a relatively-shallow lake with some water less
than 12-inches deep and rarely over 20-foot deep, with most
of the water 6- to 8-foot deep. Because of the abundance
of structure and brush in the lake, a first-timer needs to
go slow in his boat and get a map to try and avoid the
stumps and learn where the channels are. The number-one
method of fishing at Reelfoot this time of year is a technique
known as spider-rigging, which gets its name because the
front end of each crappie boat is rigged with pole holders
with eight poles out the front of the boat with lines down in
the water, making the boat resemble a spider's web. Spider-
rigging is basically slow-trolling for crappie. Anglers often
use slip corks to spin their minnows just above the stumps
and logs they're trolling over. The rate of speed is critically
important. "We'll often troll from 1/2-mile per hour up to
as much as 2-miles per hour when the crappie are feeding
aggressively," Blakely says.

Because speedometers on boats are rarely sensitive
enough to report speeds of less than 5-miles an hour,
Blakely and the other spider-riggers on Reelfoot use hand-
held GPS receivers or use the GPS receivers in their depth
finders. Blakely grew up on Reelfoot Lake, so he knows
where all the stump beds are. "In the early part of the spring,
like right now, we'll use live minnows about 1-1/2-inches
long. I like the smaller minnows, since that's the size of
the bait in the lake, and I've found that I can catch big
crappie using little minnows at this time of the year. We use
a double-hook minnow rig on the end of fiberglass poles that
are out in front of the boat. When the cork goes down I'll
give it a quick jerk, set the hook and bring the crappie on-
board."

31

Because March and the first of April are always windy months, Blakely and the other guides out of Blue Bank Resort use chains, windsocks and anchors to control the speed of their boats. Windsocks are not very common in the South, but they're often used in the big waters of the Great Lakes to control the speed of the boats. The chain that the guides use to control their boats is a very-interesting idea. "We use big chains that are about 4- to 5-feet long," Blakely says. "We replace the anchor on an electric anchor with a chain. Depending on how strong the wind is, we can let the chain down to the bottom. The faster the boat is being pushed by the wind, the more links of chain we have dragging the bottom. If the wind is light, we only let down a few links of the chain. This way we can control the speed of the boat in a heavy wind."

On the days when there is little or no wind, Blakely uses a trolling motor to increase or decrease the speed at which he trolls. When he finds a school of crappie, he can let out more chain to stop the boat or pull on the anchor rope to back the boat up and hold it at the spot where he's finding the crappie. Most of the guides at Reelfoot have been fishing the lake all their lives. They know what baits a crappie will take probably before the crappie knows. They know where to find the crappie, how they're positioned on the structure, and what tactic is required to catch the crappie every day of the year. One of the reasons I like to fish with Blakely and the other guides on this lake is to continue my education in crappie fishing. You can learn more about how to find and catch crappie in a day of fishing with these guides than you can in 3 or 4 years of trying to learn how to catch crappie on your own.

Billy Blakely Says to Bet on Black Crappie Year-Round at Reelfoot Lake

The black crappie has to be one of the prettiest crappie that swims. When it's all colored-up in the spring of the year, it's a beautiful fish, fun to catch and delicious to eat but he's a fish of mystery. The black crappie likes the shade and the shallow water and is an ambush feeder. It blends in well with the underwater environment where the fish lives and feeds. One of the ways to tell the difference between a black crappie and a white crappie is that the black crappie

34

has six anal spines and seven to eight dorsal spines. The
white crappie has only six dorsal spines. The black crappie
ranges from south Manitoba to the upper St. Lawrence River
in Quebec, then south through Nebraska to western
Pennsylvania, northern Texas and southern Florida, north
along the Atlantic Coast to North Carolina. The black
crappie also have been introduced further north along the
Atlantic drainages, and introductions have been made in
the West and as far north as British Columbia. You can
catch white crappie in rough water and swift current, but
the black crappie prefers quiet water and more vegetation
than the white crappie does. The black crappie also travels
in schools, and you rarely see as many black crappie as you
do white crappie.

At Reelfoot Lake you can catch black crappie all year
long. However, black crappie spawn earlier than the white
crappie and generally prefer much-more shallow water.
They are relatively easy to catch during the spawn, but after
the spawn occurs, Blakely says, "To catch them, you have
to bump jigs off their noses." Because the black crappie will
spawn first, the spawning season for this fish usually occurs
from the middle to the end of March. Instead of spider-
rigging, Blakely prefers to fish with 14-foot poles with small
jigs and drop-fish around the lily pads. "I like the longer
fiberglass poles to get the jig further away from the boat
and farther into the lily pads than I can reach with a shorter
pole. We often can catch a limit of black crappie fairly easily
before the weather gets too hot, and before they leave the
shallow water."

One of the advantages of crappie fishing at Reelfoot is
that you can tell the guide whether you prefer to catch black
crappie, white crappie or catch crappie of any color. As far

as the fight and the flavor of the meat, both types of crappie are equally fun to fish for and delicious to eat.

How to Find and Catch White Crappie with Reelfoot Lake's Billy Blakely

The white crappie spawns after the black crappie. There are several distinguishing characteristics that help you identify the white crappie from the black crappie. The white crappie is the only member of the sunfish family that has six spines in its dorsal fin and six spines in its anal fin. Also the spots on the side of the white crappie are arranged in seven to nine vertical bars, while the spots on the black crappie are scattered. The sides of the white crappie are silver and olive and fade into an olive green on its back. The white crappie is generally longer and has a high-arching back in comparison to the black crappie. The white crappie also is often called a calico or white perch and the fishermen in Louisiana often call the white crappie "sac-a-lait, loosely translated as sack of milk." The average white crappie will be 6- to 12-inches long and weigh less than a pound. However, 2- to 3-pound crappie aren't that uncommon, and some have been reported weighing 5 pounds. You'll find white crappie holding over hard and soft bottoms, and recent technology has shown that they often hold-out in open water, suspended during the summer and winter months. One of the newest devices to make finding white crappie much easier, especially when they're suspended, is side-scanning sonar (depth finders).

"On a side-scanner, the crappie will light-up like little Christmas trees when they're holding on brush or stumps," Blakely reports. "You'll often see them under schools of bait when they're in open water." Billy Blakely has learned the technique for locating white crappie much like he finds turkeys. "I go out on the lake the afternoon before I'm going to fish the next morning and look for shad flipping on the surface. Generally wherever those shad are late in the afternoon is where they'll be the following morning, and that's where the crappie will be. Finding crappie before you fish for them is much like hunting turkeys. If you find where the turkey is gobbling from the roost the night before you try to hunt that turkey the following morning, you've got every reason to believe that that gobbler will be where he's roosted the previous night. We've got a lot of stumps, logs and brush in Reelfoot Lake, but not all of these will be holding crappie. The one thing that crappie has to have more than anything else is food. Therefore, wherever you pinpoint the baitfish is usually where you'll find the crappie.

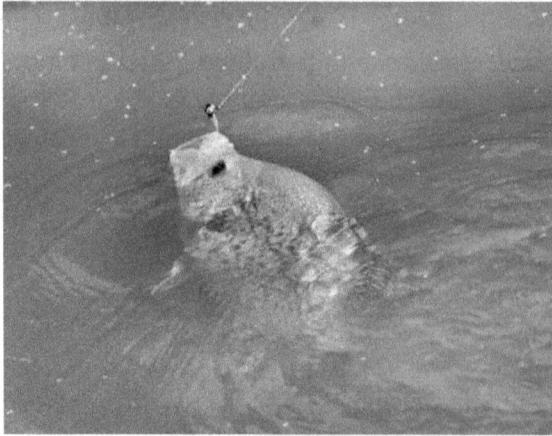

Billy Blakely Explains Where to Find the Crappie after the Spawn at Tennessee's Reelfoot Lake

By the middle of May or the first of June in many areas, crappie fishermen usually vanish, because they don't know where to find the crappie or how to catch them. But that's not true on Reelfoot Lake in northwestern Tennessee. "After the spawn, the crappie move-out of the shallow water to the stumps in deeper water," Blakely says. "This is when the crappie gang-up on large rows of stumps. They're not going to move very much, so you have to fish right on top of the stumps where the crappie are holding. You have to put that bait right in front of the fish." In a day of fishing Blakely often will take 15-dozen minnows, troll very slowly and move-onto the spot he wants to fish, then back-off and move-onto it again. At this time of the year, if you find a good school of crappie, Blakely suggests that you

continue to fish that school. What many fishermen don't
realize is that crappie don't bite all day long. Who knows
why they decide to bite, and whey they decide not to bite,
but Blakely suggests you keep your bait in front of them,
until the crappie decides to bite. You may go from famine to
feast when the crappie start biting every time you drop a bait
in front of them. Once again remember that crappie have
to be where the baitfish are holding. Locating the baitfish
becomes very important.

Because the guides at Blue Bank Resort are on the
water all day every day, they stay in touch with where
the crappie are holding, when they're biting, and how big
the fish are that are running. "On a good day during May
and June, we can often get a limit of 90 crappie for three
anglers, or 60, which is two limits for two anglers," Blakely
mentions. However, fishing is still fishing. Some days the
crappie may get lockjaw, and you may not load the boat.
One of the advantages you have at Blue Bank Resort is that
if you're having a hard time finding and catching crappie
by yourself, Blakely will take a break in his day and show
you where you can catch crappie and how to fish for those
crappies. "My job here at Blue Bank is to help everyone I
can catch all the crappie they want to catch. People keep
coming-back to Blue Bank Resort and Reelfoot Lake,
because they continue to catch crappie here. We do
everything we can to help them be successful."

Another reason people come to Blue Bank to fish Reelfoot is because the resort has very-nice accommodations and amenities, besides delicious meals, including prime rib, crab cakes, the old standby – catfish, and many-other delicious entrees. "We're also one of the few restaurants on the lake that will cook your catch," says Mike Hayes with Blue Bank Resort. "You can come in from fishing, and we have people available to clean your fish while you shower and get ready for dinner. When you come-down to eat, the fish you've just caught will be prepared with plenty of delicious side dishes and whatever you want to drink."

There is one caution I should warn you about before dinner at Blue Bank. Most of the time, you'll be served hot rolls and strawberry butter before the meal. Once you start eating those hot rolls and strawberry butter, you'll be hard-pressed to stop eating them. As a matter of fact, I couldn't finish a delicious, cooked-on-the-grill prime rib, because I'd eaten too-many rolls and strawberry butter.

Billy Blakely Recommends You Fish Crankbaits for Crappie

Many years ago when I fished out of a rented, wooden johnboat that came equipped with an empty dog-food can to be used to bail the water from the boat as it leaked, my dad and I were trolling crankbaits to catch spotted bass on Smith Lake. All of a sudden I had a big bite, but the fish on the other end of the rod didn't jump and didn't fight like a bass. When I got the fish up to the side of the boat, I'd landed a 2-pound crappie. I never had seen a crappie take a crankbait. I really didn't think that much about it, because I didn't catch another crappie on a crankbait for many years. But tournament crappie fishermen have been using crankbaits to catch crappie for the last decade. However, most of these crankbaits have been small bass crankbaits that they have put about a foot or two up the line on the poles they've used to troll. On the bottoms of the lines, they've used weights, often as much as an ounce, to get the crankbaits down to the depth they want to troll. In years past, these crankbaits have come in colors designed to catch bass. But, one of the hottest colors for catching crappie in the summertime is a pink crankbait, which more lure manufacturers now are producing for fishermen who troll crankbaits for crappie in the summertime. In recent years, both Strike King and Bandit have stepped to the forefront in designing and painting crankbaits to meet the needs of hot-weather crappie fishermen.

"We troll those crankbaits through the stumps and the logs up here at Reelfoot and catch crappie all summer long," Blakely explains. "Yes, we'll get a few crankbaits hung. But we catch a lot of crappie. Many people don't know how effective trolling crankbaits for crappie can be, until they try it. That's one of the advantages we have here at Reelfoot is that there is no time of year that we can't catch crappie using some type of tactic."

Even in the fall and the winter months when the Reelfoot sportsman's attention turns to waterfowl hunting, many of the guides take their duck hunters crappie fishing after they've filled their limit of webfoots. "Plenty of days during duck season, I'll take clients out before daylight, and they'll get their limit of ducks by 8:00 or 9:00 am, come-in, eat lunch and then go-out and catch their limit of crappie before the day is over," Blakely reports. "Crappie bite all year long, and you can catch crappie all year long, if you know where and how to fish for them, know the baits they want to take and how to present those baits to the crappie, so they'll eat them."

A day on the water with Billy Blakely is like going to college on crappie. Blakely fishes all year long and almost every day. I think sometimes the crappie in Reelfoot call Billy Blakely at night to find out where they're supposed to be the next day.

Chapter 4 - How Weather Conditions Affect Springtime Crappie Fishing with John Woods

Editor's Note: John Woods of Newbern, Tennessee, and his partner, Tracy MacIntosh, of Dyersburg, Tenn., are two of the strongest tournament crappie anglers on the national circuit. When not fishing in tournaments, Woods is guiding crappie fishermen on all of the north Mississippi lakes, including Grenada, Enid, Sardis and Arkabutler. He also guides on Kentucky Lake and Reelfoot Lake. He likes to fish the northwest Mississippi lakes, because he generally can catch more and bigger crappie in the hot summer months there. Anyone can catch crappie when the water's stable, the wind's calm, and the fish are biting. But what do you do when weather conditions are against you?

Fishing for Crappie in Changing Water and Weather Conditions

Question: John, one spring when you went to Enid Lake in northern Mississippi, the water was coming-up, the wind was blowing, the temperature was cold, the water was muddy, and you hadn't fished that lake in several years. How did you find and catch crappie?

Woods: Anytime I go to a lake I haven't fished very much, I use one of two tactics to find crappie. I first look for drop-offs, like creek channels, underwater bluffs or rivers or ditches. Usually on a drop like a creek channel, you either can find natural brush, like stumps and logs or man-made brush piles or stake beds. When I went to Lake Enid a couple of weeks ago, the lake had been low, but it had experienced a lot of rain and had risen several feet before we arrived. Generally, when you get that much fresh water coming into a lake, like we usually see after spring rains and floods, crappie usually move up with the rising water.

Crappie like to move into freshly-flooded grass and flooded trees or bushes (my second spot to search for crappie on a new lake). Oftentimes, if the waters really rise, like at Enid Lake, it's often the first place I look. Crappie like rising water, and biologists have learned that crappie get off their best spawns during the years when there are floods or extremely-high water. We had two problems at Enid – really-high winds, which can cause us not to be able to fish the way we want, and rising water, which is a good thing.

To get out of the wind, I went down beside the dam and found grass in about 2-1/2-feet of water. The crappie had moved up into the grass in that shallow water. The depth finder only recorded 1-1/2-feet of water, which most people think is too shallow to be able to fish. But if you have your depth finder's transducer mounted on the foot of your trolling motor, it's at least 1-to 1-1/2-feet deeper than where the depth finder indicates you're located. When my depth finder showed that I was fishing in 1-1/2-feet of water, I knew I was really fishing in 2-1/2-feet of water. The water temperature was about 57 degrees and warming. The crappie had spawning on their mind. So, I put out six poles on the front of the boat, each with a jig and a minnow about 1-1/2-feet down in the water. With my jigs 1-1/2-feet from the surface, the crappie still had 1 foot of water where they could be holding close to the bottom, and that's where we found and caught the crappie.

Question: John you were fishing spotty grasses with a patch of grass here and there. Why did you decide to use 12-foot trolling poles rather than fishing with a hand pole?

Woods: Because the grass was spotty, I knew there was grass under my boat that I couldn't see. I've learned that when I troll from spot to spot, I'm fishing over grass that may hold crappie in-between the mats of grass I can see. Even when I'm fishing trees and bushes, I always troll between the two areas I'll be targeting, because most of the time there's structure underwater you can't see between the two pieces of cover you can see. Many people only fish the structure they can see. I like to fish structure I can see, but I prefer to fish structure I can't see. In Lake Enid, if you can see patches of grass scattered along the shoreline, it generally means there's grass under the water you can't see. Therefore, if you can catch crappie around the surface where you can see, you should be able to catch crappie around the grass you can't see.

Question: Also at Enid, the weather was cool. It had been warm 1 or 2 days before you arrived, but there was a cold front moving onto the lake. Why did you continue to fish shallow?

Woods: The weather wouldn't run the crappie off the banks and out of the shallow water because the new water was coming into the lake, and the crappie were moving up in the new water and concentrating in grass in only 2-1/2- to 3 feet of water. If I could put the minnows and the jigs above the crappie's heads, they'd eat my baits. And, it worked. The crappie were there, and we caught them. I like the longer 12-foot poles, because they keep the baits further out and away from the boat. If you have a partner with a dip net, you only have to back the poles up and your partner can net your fish right off the front of the boat. Weather conditions don't really change the fishing that much. It takes the fish 1 or 2 days to adjust to any kind of weather change, and even then, they'll still be around the same place you found them before the weather change.

Fishing for Crappie after a Spring Rain and a Freaky Cold Front

Question: John, weather changes often will throw a fisherman a curve when he's trying to find and catch crappie. Let's say you're fishing in a tournament, and you've had stable weather right up until the night before the tournament when a huge rain storm comes in with thunder and lighting, bringing a lot of new water into the lake and muddying it up. How do you find and catch crappie then?

Woods: Wherever I've found my fish in practice is where I'll fish. The lake may have risen and become stained, but the crappie haven't left the area. The crappie still will be in the same spot where I've found them. So, that's where I'll look for crappie on the tournament day. The crappie may have moved over, up or down a few feet, but they'll still be in that same general region. If I've been fishing in clear water, but because of rain, the water has become stained, I'll fish a bigger bait. I may use a 2- or a 2-1/2-inch jig with a 3-inch live minnow behind that jig. The more stained the water, the bigger the bait I'll use. The bigger the bait, the easier it is for the crappie to see.

Question: Okay, John, let's say you're fishing pretty weather with a 60- to a 70-degree air temperature, and the temperature even may rise to the 80s. You go to bed that night confident that you'll be slaying crappie in the morning under bluebird skies and warm weather. However, when you wake up, one of those freaky cold fronts like many parts of the country have endured the first 2 weeks of April may have come through, dropping the temperature down to 20 or 30 degrees. You may have to wear your snowmobile suit over the top of your shorts and t-shirt to keep from getting hypothermia. How will the cold front affect the crappie?

Woods: The crappie won't move drastically, but they may be somewhat deeper and more reluctant to bite. So if the bite's slow, I'll slow down my presentation. If I'm trolling, I'll troll slower than when the water is warmer. I may even give the fish a slower presentation with a hand pole. Fishing with a hand pole is my most-favorite way to fish. But when you're fishing tournaments, you have to put those eight poles out and troll to be competitive. When that cold weather hits, and the fish won't bite, I find underwater structure and bang my jigs and minnows on it until I can make those crappie bite.

Question: When you're fishing with a hand pole, what size hand pole do you use?

Woods: Most of the time I'm fishing with a 10-foot B'nM pole, because it's extremely sensitive, yet strong enough to bring up a crappie to the top where it can be netted. On the back of my 10-foot pole, on the very butt of the pole, I mount a spinning reel. Many times Tracy, my favorite fishing partner, and I will use Martin automatic reels. When you push the trigger on that reel, it automatically starts winding-up on your line. That's a real asset when you're fishing deep. As soon as you feel the bite, set the hook, and push the trigger on the reel, and the crappie will be on its way to the surface.

Beating a Bad Wind and Heavy Rain

Question: John, we've talked about how to deal with rising lakes, muddy water and cold fronts, but another weather condition that really throws many crappie fishermen a curve is wind. How do you deal with windy conditions when you're trying to catch crappie?

Woods: First, I try to find a creek or a high bank where I've pre-fished that will break the wind and allow me to fish the way I want. When I fished on Enid Lake in Mississippi recently, I got behind the dam wall, which broke the wind, allowing me to fish in calm water. But when Tracy MacIntosh, my crappie-tournament partner from Dyersburg, Tenn., and I have found crappie out in a main lake before, and we've caught them by trolling, we'll put out our drift sock that will hold us against the wind and slow-down our boat. Then we can troll at the speed we want. Remember, the drift sock won't stop your boat. It just slows-down the boat. If we want to completely stop the boat, we'll let out a chain tied to a rope behind the boat. Then we use our trolling motor to pull us forward against the chain, so we can move at the speed we want to move. We have different sizes and lengths of chains that we can let out behind the boat, depending on how strong the wind's blowing. If we want to stay in one position, the chain will hold us where we want to fish, and if we want to move up a little bit, we turn the trolling motor on enough to move us as far as we need. Sometimes we'll tie the rope holding the chain to the pedestal seat on the front of the boat. This way, we can reach down, untie the rope, pull the chain forward some, let the rope out and then inch-up to a piece of cover we want to fish.

Question: Why did you decide to use a chain instead of another form of anchor?

Woods: The chain doesn't hang in the bottom like other anchor types will. Many fishermen try to use iron window weights, but those weights tend to hang-up more than a chain does. The chain will snake itself around different types of cover in the water. For instance, with a little help from the trolling motor, the chain will work itself through logs, tree limbs and rocks without hanging up.

Question: How do you decide whether you'll use a chain or a windsock? And, have you ever used both?

Woods: Yes, I have used both. The windsock's good in a slight breeze or a general blowing wind, but in a heavy wind, you'll need the chain. The heavier the wind, the bigger and the longer the chain you want to use. By using the chain and the trolling motor, we can adjust the trolling speed at which our boat travels to troll our jigs at the speed we've determined the crappie want to bite them. We always move with the wind and are moved by the wind, rather than trying to go into the wind. As long as the waves aren't big enough to sink the boat, Tracy and I can fish.

Question: John, how do you handle rain? If you've practiced with clear skies, but you wake up at a crappie tournament to find the rain's pouring down, how do you adjust?

Woods: We put on our rain suits and go fishing. We don't change our fishing style because of the rain. Now, if the rain has lightning in it, then we'll get off the water. But in a pouring rain, Tracy and I fish like we always do. There are only two things that will make me go to the bank: lightning and a wind high enough to sink the boat. I remember one tournament Tracy and I were fishing when a freaky front came through with a lot of static electricity, but no lightning or rain. Our B'n'M graphite poles started crackling and sounding like they were frying. When we tried to touch them, there would be an arc of electricity between our fingertips and the poles. When we started to pick the poles up, they'd shock us. I told Tracy we must have a short in the trolling motor.

I'd never had anything like that happen to me in all my years of fishing. When we returned to the weigh-in site and were standing in line to weigh our fish, I mentioned the short in the trolling motor to one of the other competitors who was waiting in line with us. He said he had the same thing happen to him and his partner. When we checked with the rest of the fishermen, we discovered about 40% of all the fishermen on the lake that day, experienced that static electricity in the air. That was about the strangest weather condition I'd ever fished. We didn't have any visible lighting, thunder or rain. We just had a freaky static-electricity front come through the area. We've fished plenty of days when the weather has been bad, and fishing hasn't been comfortable, but we've learned how to overcome all kinds of weather conditions and keep-on fishing for crappie.

Chapter 5 - Where and How to Fish for May Crappie

Fishing a Lake with Current in May with Steve Coleman

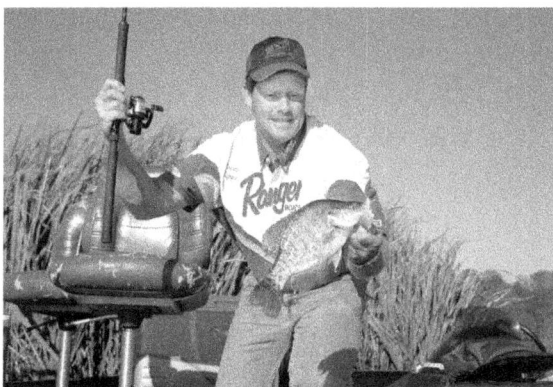

Editor's Note: Steve Coleman of Tennessee and his partner, Ronnie Capps, are two of the most-successful tournament crappie fishermen in the nation. Coleman will tell us how he finds May crappie in a lake with current.

Question: Steve, how do you locate crappie in May in a lake with current?

Coleman: First, Ronnie and I search for structure and then check the structure for crappie. Current running through a lake carries oxygen. The crappie can hold really deep, if the lake's deep, and current's being pulled through it. For instance, Ronnie and I caught crappie 60-feet deep at J. Percy Priest Lake in Nashville, Tennessee. There was plenty of good structure and oxygen at that depth, but no fishing pressure. As long as crappie have enough oxygen to survive and good cover, the depth of water they hold in doesn't really matter.

Question: Are the crappie always deep after the spawn and into the summer?

Coleman: No, they can be really shallow. If baitfish are holding in shallow water, that's where the crappie will be, too. So, in the hot summer months, numbers of crappie are caught on crankbaits in water depths of 12 feet or less. The crappie will move up into the more-shallow water, even in the summertime, to feed on schools of baitfish.

Question: Steve, after the spawn, the crappie can become really tough to catch for a couple of weeks. When's that time frame on Reelfoot Lake where you and Ronnie live?

Coleman: Generally, it occurs from the middle of May until the first of June. On Reelfoot, at this time of year, the bluegills start spawning. So, we also can use our poles to catch bluegills, even if the crappie fishing gets tough.

Question: Does that mean that you and Ronnie stop fishing when the crappie are difficult to catch?

Coleman: No, not at all. That's when we have to make the crappie bite.

Question: Okay, how do you make crappie bite when they don't want to bite?

Coleman: We fish with lighter tackle. We'll be fishing 6-pound-test line and a 1/16- or a 1/32-ounce jig with a really-small minnow. Remember that the crappie that have come through the spawn will be skinny and not feeling very good. We'll still be trolling with poles, and if the water's muddy, we'll move-up to 8-pound-test line. Most of the time we'll be trolling with 6-pound-test line and a 1/16-ounce jig with a minnow. Our favorite colors are the MidSouth Green and Chartreuse Glow jigs. We'll primarily be trolling over creek channels, drop-offs and ledges. About this time of year, the thicker the brush we fish, the more crappie we catch.

In May, crappie are looking for brush they can call home until they get over the effects of the spawn. So, if you want to catch the crappie and make them bite when they're not biting, you'll have to get down in that brush or troll over the top of that brush. Just because crappie fishing will be tough in our area from the middle of May to the first of June doesn't mean the crappie can't be caught. You'll just need to use smaller lines, baits and minnows and fish thicker cover.

Dock Shooting Docks in May with Russ Bailey

Editor's Note: Russ Bailey of St. Mary's Ohio, is a guide and often appears on TV shows, besides fishing crappie tournaments. He's found the tactic of shooting docks in May very-productive.

As the weather warms-up the shallow bays, dock shooting can be one of the most-productive and fun ways to catch crappie. I've had the pleasure of fishing with some of the best guides and tournament pros in the country, who have shared their favorite crappie-catching techniques with me. But shooting docks is still my favorite way to crappie fish. I learned this technique several years ago from Jack Jones, former owner of the Bay Springs Marina on beautiful Weiss Lake in Alabama. This tactic has helped me qualify for most of the 10 Crappie Classics I've fished.

There are different ways to shoot docks, depending on the water depth, the time of year and the aggressiveness of the crappie. Most of the docks I fish, whether in the North or the South, are normally in about 6 to 10 feet of water. Many of these docks are huge, have posts going into the water and brush buried under them – all of which gives the crappie plenty of shade, cover and baitfish.

The Equipment You Need

Getting started with equipment is simple. I like two rods for shooting docks – the B'n'M 5-1/2-foot Sharpshooter and the B'n'M Buck's Graphite 6-1/2-foot Crappie Spinning Rod. For fishing the shallow-water docks, I generally use a 1/48-ounce minnow lead head with Southern Pro's Hot Crappie Stingers or Lit'l Hustlers. Sometimes using a cork just big enough to hold-up a jig is the most-productive way to fish. When I'm cork fishing, I use 6-pound-test clear Sufix Siege line tied snug to the jig head. If I'm shooting without a cork, I like using the neon tangerine or high-vis yellow line. I'll also use a loop knot, when fishing without a cork.

If you've never fished this way, practice before going to the water. The easiest way to practice is to set up a kitchen chair in the yard. Start by shooting under the chair, between the legs. When you can accomplish this with ease, then try to actually hit the chair legs. When you first start, pull the jig back, and hold it only by the head of the jig. I've seen anglers pull back by their hooks and eventually get stuck. With your pole hand, open your bail, and just let the line rest on your index finger. As you release the jig, the line will easily come off your finger and bail.

Here's the rule of thumb for choosing to fish with a cork or without one. Normally in the spring, especially in the

North, cold fronts are very frequent. A one-day 20-degree temperature change isn't unusual, which can cause the fish to be more finicky. A cork really helps in this type of fishing situation. Once you learn the depth at which the crappie are holding under the dock, you can set your cork accordingly. I use a small fly cork that's only big enough to hold-up my jig. I've watched fishermen with big corks or bobbers receive subtle hits by crappie and never realize they've had fish on their lines. Even with the small corks, there are times when the crappie won't take the bait. Sometimes, the cork will lie on its side or move just slightly. With a big cork, these types of hits can go unnoticed. To avoid problems on windy days, break-off all but a small piece of the toothpick on the cork, stopping the line from wrapping around it.

When you shoot the jig back under the dock, you can really slow-down your presentation, which also keeps the jig in the strike zone of the bass the entire time you work it back toward you. The key is to pop the jig slightly one or two times and then let it sit still for several seconds, which is when you'll get most of your strikes. When you move the jig, it gets the crappie's attention, and as the jig sits still, the fish will hit it. Overworking the jig is a big mistake. Also, when you set the hook, make your initial hook set a big one, and then let the drag do the work for you. A hard hook set will put the jig in the top of the crappie's mouth, which is the hardest part.

If the fish are a little deeper under the docks, even close to the bottom, or they're very aggressive, this is the time to shoot without the cork. For this technique, use the high-vis line because line watching is critical. If you wait for the feel of the crappie on the line, many times, it will be too late. When you shoot the jig under a dock, and it begins to fall, look for the line to jump or move differently than it usually does. If this happens, set the hook immediately. Many times, when you first learn to shoot docks, keeping the jig in the strike zone is hard. If you retrieve the jig too high, the fish may not give chase, and they won't hit any jigs below them. I'll use a Southern Pro Hot Grub for this retrieve.

If you've ever played any type of sports, you know that the only way to get better is to practice, which is also true in fishing. Watching TV shows and reading articles can give you tips and techniques, but nothing can replace time on the water. To be a better angler, you have to get out there and learn how to get the fish to bite. Remember, the tough days can be the best to learn, because you really have to work to figure out what will work to get the crappie in the boat. If you've never tried dock shooting, give it a try. I'm sure you'll enjoy it as much as I do.

Shooting and Trolling Docks on Alabama's Weiss Lake with Darrell Baker in May

Editor's Note: Many crappie fishermen like to shoot docks to catch crappie. And usually the crappie are under the docks, but sometimes they're not. But where are the fish when they're not under the docks? Darrell Baker, who has been fishing Alabama's Weiss Lake for more than three

62

decades and guiding on the lake for almost a decade, answers this question.

Question: Darrell, what are you using to shoot docks?

Baker: I like the 5-1/2-foot B 'n' M SharpShooter. I shoot a 1/24-ounce jig made by Southern Pro called the Crappie Stinger.

Question: How do you find the crappie when the crappie aren't under the docks?

Baker: My fishing clients and I will move from one dock to the next dock, and we leave our jigs hanging in the water as I use the trolling motor to move to the next dock. One time as I was moving, one of my clients caught a crappie, and then I did. I decided crappie must be suspending out in front of the docks before they moved under the docks. I also figured that since we were moving the boat when we caught those two crappie that the crappie out in front of the docks could be caught trolling. On my next trip, I rigged-up all my trolling poles and racks and started trolling in front of the docks I planned to shoot.

In late May, we've caught crappie trolling in front of the docks when we can't catch the crappie shooting the docks. What I've learned is that often early in the morning and late in the afternoon on bright, sunny days, the crappie will pull out from under the docks and suspend in front of the docks. That's the time you can catch them trolling. But later in the morning, when the sun climbs high, and the day gets brighter, the crappie that have been suspending in front of the docks actually will move under the docks in the shade. Then they can hold more comfortably and catch and eat more bait. I've found that on a combination trip of trolling and dock shooting, we catch more crappie using the two techniques at different times of day than we do when we stick to one tactic. Trolling until 10:00 or 11:00 am in front of the docks can be highly productive. But then when the sun gets high in the sky, I'll pull in my trolling rods, take down my trolling racks and start dock shooting. We often can catch as many, if not more crappie, by shooting the docks as we did trolling in front of the docks. Whenever the trolling bite slows down, I realize that the crappie have moved away from that open water and under those docks. So I don't really watch my watch. Instead, I watch my trolling poles, and when the action stops on the poles, we start shooting docks.

Question: How long will the dock shooting and trolling in front of the docks produce crappie?

Baker: Depending on the weather and the water, this tactic usually will produce through the first two weeks of June. But that timetable is on Weiss Lake. I believe if you're successfully catching crappie by shooting docks, during the early morning and late afternoon you may want to try trolling in front of the docks you've been shooting and catching crappie. Then switch to your dock-shooting tactic when the sun gets up, and the trolling bite drops off. At least, that's what I've learned, and that's what's working for me.

Chapter 6 - What You Can Learn from Professional Bassers Ken Cook and Tony Stacy about Fishing for Summertime Crappie

Editor's Note: Ken Cook of Meers, Oklahoma, a former fisheries biologist, longtime professional bass fisherman and avid crappie fisherman, shares his methods for finding and catching crappie in the summertime. And Tony Stacy of Andalusia, Alabama, who tournament fishes the Wal-Mart Bass Fishing League (WBL) does too.

Ken Cook on Ways to Take Summertime Crappie

"If you want to take crappie in the summertime, you must learn how to use your depth finder and locate the fish in open water, because that's what summertime crappie fishing is all about," Cook says. Cook enjoys the crappie fishing anytime, but particularly in the middle of the day during the summertime to provide a break for him when he finds mid-day fishing for largemouth bass tough. After the spawn, crappie move to deep water, which is when most anglers have a difficult time catching them. "When crappie come off the bank to move to deep water, they often become edge feeders- swimming and holding along various edges like ledges and drop-offs," Cook reports.

Find the pH Breakline and the Thermocline

As Cook explains, "The drop-offs along major creek and river channels often are the best places to locate crappie during the summer months. The pH breakline will show us where the ideal pH is, and the thermocline will denote where the ideal water temperature is. Usually, the pH breakline will sit right on top of the thermocline. To locate these breaklines, I use a pH meter and find at what depth I get a pH and a temperature breakline. There's another method of identifying this breakline where not only crappie and bass but just about all the fish in a lake hold on, and that's by running your boat across the lake and taking note at what depth you spot fish showing up on your depth finder. By averaging the depths where you see the most fish, you reasonably can assume that this is the thermocline and pH breakline."

Locate a Bottom Break

The bottom break is an edge that the crappie will travel along. If you can locate a place where it intersects the water depth where the proper pH and thermocline are, you'll know the water depth the crappie will be the most comfortable in and then you can find the ledge where they want to feed."

Pinpoint Cover

"I define cover as some kind of brush, stumps, logs or anything that the crappie can lie next to, get under or get inside of," Cook mentions. "I use these three ingredients like a road map. I locate the water temperature and thermocline the crappie prefer first. Next I follow that water temperature line until I intersect structure. Then I follow that structure until I discover cover. This simple, basic formula will aid you in locating crappie on any lake the same way bass anglers find bass in the summertime."

Fish with Light Tackle

"During the summer months, the crappie fisherman needs to use smaller baits and lighter tackle," Cook reports. "When you catch one crappie, you usually can assume there are more crappie in the area."

Use a Depth Finder

In the summertime, crappie may hold in and under cover and not show up on a depth finder. "Crappie tend to school at a particular depth, according to water temperature and dissolved oxygen content," Cook emphasizes. Many times if the crappie aren't in the cover, they'll be schooled-up above or under the cover or off to the side of it."

According to Dr. Tom Forsyth, who has a PhD in fishery biology, "When you discover a school of fish like this in the summer, you can assume several things about them. Vertical jigging or fishing deep with minnows right on top of the schools will be the best method to catch these crappie. They won't come away from the cover to take the bait. You can return to that same school for several days without the school's having moved. What actually happens in the summertime is the amount of water the crappie can survive in shrinks drastically. Therefore the crappie have to be concentrated in larger schools to survive. To locate crappie, an angler must utilize a depth finder. However, he'll have to look in much less water for the fish than he did during the post-spawn time of the year when the water conditions were better for the crappie. The advantage to summertime fishing for crappie is that if an angler can fish consecutively for 3 or 4 days, he can go to the same places where he's located the schools and continue to catch fish out of those schools all 3 days. If an angler learns how to take crappie in the summer, he consistently can catch more fish than he will during the spring when the crappie go to the banks, because the crappie are more concentrated in the summer than they are in springtime."

Talk to Bass Fishermen

"When bass anglers fish points, ledges, drop-offs, deep cover and structure, they often will have numbers of small pecks on their plastic worms or crankbaits," Cook explains. "More than likely these strikes are either crappie or bluegills that haven't been caught. Crappie often will try to kill and

eat a bait too big for them to swallow and will attack the
larger lures that bass anglers fish.

Talk to bass fishermen, and ask about places where they
have had numbers of light bites. Then go to that same area
with your light line and crappie lures or live minnows, and
you easily may come home with a limit of crappie."

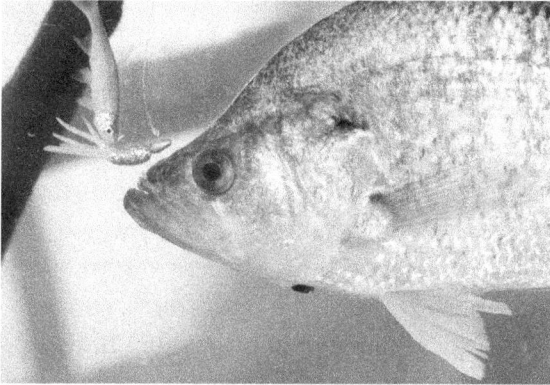

Determine the Best Bait

Cook prefers to fish small jigs weighing from 1/16- to
1/32-ounce each. "I like 4- to 6- pound line, and I fish the
little jigs on a slow, steady retrieve," Cook reports. "Crappie
don't like a hopping or a jerking type of retrieve, but prefer
a slower, easier-to-catch bait. Of course in hot weather,
crappie may be ornery about hitting any bait. If this tactic
doesn't work, the bait of last resort for me is the live
minnow. Even a crappie that doesn't want to feed and isn't
hungry just has to hit a live minnow swimming in front of
its nose."

Set the Hook Properly

"Setting the hook correctly is important, too, in catching crappie," Cook advises. "As soon as you feel the slightest twitch on the line, set the hook. However, since crappie have tender mouths, don't set the hook too hard, or you'll lose the fish. Most of the time when you feel the bite, the crappie already has taken the bait."

Fish Bridge Pilings and Railroad Trestles

"During the hot summer months, these vertical structures that go from the bottom to above the surface allow a crappie to hold in any depth of water in which it wants to hold," Cooke explains. "Plus if there's current coming through the lake, the bridge pilings offer a current break where baitfish and crappie can hold. Fishing bridge pilings either by day or night can pay major crappie dividends for the summertime crappie angler."

Utilize Buoys

"Once you locate the proper water depth with the right temperature and correct amount of oxygen content that intersects a creek or a river channel, you can buoy off 200 to 300 yards of the edge of the old creek channel and then motor your boat between your buoys," Cook explains. "Although crappie prefer to hold on cover, large schools of crappie will travel up and down these edges, feeding, swimming together and moving from location to location. When you see a school of fish on your depth finder between the buoys you have out, drop another buoy to mark the school. Then go back, and fish for the crappie in each school that you've marked. When one school of crappie quits biting, move to the next buoy, and fish for another school. After you've fished all the schools you've marked, and the fish have stopped biting, you can pick up your buoys, run the same 100 yards of underwater creek bank, often relocate the schools, rebuoy them off and continue to fish. Or, mark another 100 yards of underwater creek bank, and repeat the same procedure. By marking the edges, searching for the crappie and buoying off the fish, anglers often can take large numbers of good-sized crappie all day long along the edge of one creek channel in the summer."

Tony Stacy Spins-Up Papermouths

"I'm a big fan of giving fish various lures, and different tactics from what they see all day, every day, on most lakes," Stacy explains. "In south Alabama, where I live, crappie are caught two ways – on live minnows or on jigs. Fishermen are using these two tactics because these two methods are the ones people always have used to catch crappie. A southerner is very traditional and often will do something because his daddy did it that way, and his daddy before him did too, so why change?

"But when I got this Mepps Panfisher Crappie Kit with five types of little spinners, including the Aglia, the Comet Mino, the Aglia Long, the Thunder Bug and the Black Fury Combo, I decided that some of them ought to catch crappie. I used 6-pound-test line and starting fishing these lures around brush piles where I thought crappie ought to hang-out. I especially liked the little Black Fury Combo. My wife and I have learned that that particular spinner in the Mepps Crappie Kit is the one that south-Alabama crappie like the best. I've found the Black Fury Combo to be most effective when the crappie are holding in shallow water as they come in to bed. I don't know whether crappie can see colors or not, but I think they can. I believe that silver blade with the red bead really gets the crappie's attention.

"My wife and I like to crappie fish, and I have to admit that sometimes she's a better crappie fisherman than I am. Another thing we've learned is that most people who have docks on a lake will have brush out in front of those docks. Very-few docks don't have brush either in front of them, under them or beside them, although this brush may not be visible from the surface. But if you start fishing those Mepps spinners around docks when crappie are near banks, you can usually brush and catch crappie.

"The crappie seem to take those Mepps spinners more readily than they will minnows and jigs, especially on lakes where they see minnows and jigs every day. I think crappie, especially the bigger crappie, wise-up to minnows and jigs more quickly than we think they do, and that's one of the reasons that I believe the Mepps spinners are often more effective than the tried-and-true methods of fishing minnows or jigs. Give these spinners a try the next time you go crappie fishing. Even if you're fishing with minnows and jigs, carry some Mepps spinners with you. When the crappie stop hitting the minnows and the jigs, you just may can start them back on a feeding spree by swimming those Mepps spinners through the area where you've been catching the crappie."

Chapter 7 - How to Longline and How to Fish Dressed Lures for Summertime Crappie

How to Longline for Crappie with Darrell Baker

Editor's Note: Darrell Baker of Centre, Alabama, has been fishing Alabama's Weiss Lake for more than 32 years and has guided on the lake for 5 years.

Question: How are you finding and catching crappie during the end of May and the first of June?

Baker: I'm finding the crappie in the mouths of spawning bays. These post-spawn crappie have moved-out of the shallow water, but they haven't made that big move to deep water yet. They've moved-out of the 2-to 3-foot-deep water out to the 7- to 11-foot-deep water. The crappie are suspended, just like prespawn crappie will be. We've had cool weather in Alabama for this time of year plus relatively-cool nights and quite a few cloudy days. So, the water temperature has remained in the mid-70s. When that water temperature moves up and gets hotter, the crappie will be headed for the main river channel and become structure-oriented on the channel edges. That's where we'll be able to catch them in the summer.

Question: How are you catching your crappie?

Baker: I'm catching them longline trolling. I'm using 10-foot and 12-foot rods on the front of the boat and 7-1/2-footers off the back of the boat. I'm fishing with 6-pound-test line and pulling 1/24-ounce jigs with Southern Pro Hot Grubs on the jigs. The best colors have been sour grape and blue chartreuse.

Question: What depth of water are you trolling?

75

Baker: The bottom's at 7- to 11-feet deep, but we're catching suspended crappie at 5 to 6 feet.

Question: What kind of structure are the crappie holding over?

Baker: I'm mainly fishing stump flats, and the crappie are holding above the stumps. But they're not real tight to the structure.

Question: In a day of crappie fishing at Weiss right now, how many crappie will you catch?

Baker: We'll usually catch over 100 crappie and keep 35-40 fish a day. In late May I average 40- to 45-keeper crappie per day. Remember that the minimum length you can keep here at Weiss Lake is 10 inches. But the crappie we've been keeping have been 11-1/2- to 12-inches each. These fish will weigh 1- to 1-1/4-pound each. We can keep 30 fish per day that are 10-inches long per person. We'll normally catch 100 to 150 crappie per day. Ninety percent of the fish we're catching are between 9- and 9-1/2-inches long, and we have to throw all those back. What's really strange is we're catching a lot of 9- and 9-1/2-inch crappie and 11- and 12-inch crappie. For some reason, we catch very few 10-inch crappie.

Question: On Weiss Lake, what water temperature do you have to have before the crappie will leave that post-spawn staging and move-out to the main river channel?

Baker: When the water temperature starts hitting 75 to 78 degrees, the crappie will start moving-out to the main river channel. That's when we find our crappie on brush piles and stumps on channel edge drops.

How to Fish Dressed Lures for Summertime Crappie Fishing with Randy Polisky

Editor's Note: Randy Polisky from Rockville, Virginia, likes to crappie fish and has been for more than 40 years.

Question: I understand you enjoy catching crappie using Mepps spinners.

Polisky: The water here in Virginia becomes very hot at times. Often during the summer months, the crappie will school-up. So, when I find a school of crappie, I use the Mepps Aglia to cast to the school. I count the Aglia as it falls, and then I start retrieving the Aglia back to the boat. When I think I've got the Aglia in the middle of the school, I kill the bait and let it fall. Now unlike bass, the crappie don't seem to take the bait on the fall, but they do take the Aglia when I start pulling up on the lure and begin to retrieve it. I think what the crappie are seeing is a baitfish about to die that drops down, and then acts like it gets another boost of energy when I start to turn the blade again. That's when the crappie will hit the Aglia. A lot of people jig for crappie, and when they do, the crappie will usually take the jig on the fall. But I've found with the Aglia, the opposite of that is true. I caught a 2-pound crappie that was 16-inches long on a dressed Mepps Aglia.

When I'm crappie fishing, I like the dressed Aglias better than the Aglias that aren't dressed. I think the dressed Aglias give the crappie a different-looking bait than what they've seen previously. If you're fishing on a lake that receives a lot of fishing pressure, those crappie have seen a jig and a minnow on a hook, but more than likely they've never seen dressed Aglias. Therefore, I think they take these lures better than lures they've seen. Even though the crappie may have seen an inline spinner or a small safety-pin spinner before, more than likely they haven't seen a dressed lure.

On the lakes that I fish, live minnows and chartreuse-colored jigs are the crappie fisherman's stock-in-trade. Those crappie see those types of baits all day, every day. But the baits they don't see are the dressed Aglias. The only other spinner bait they've probably seen is the Beetle Spin, a small safety-pin-type spinner with a little grub on it. Therefore, I know they haven't seen anything close to the dressed Aglia, and I believe that's the reason it's so deadly-effective against crappie.

Question: Why did you decide to start using Mepps spinners for crappie?

Polisky: I watched that Mepps spinner coming through the water and decided that it looked like a little minnow. I knew that crappie liked flash and color. So, I started playing with the dressed Aglia, and I started catching crappie. I caught enough crappie on the Aglia to build confidence in it, and now I fish it regularly to catch crappie. Most fishermen have their favorite lures that they always use. These lures are their favorites because they've caught so many fish on them. However, I believe this is a self-fulfilling prophecy. In other words, they catch so many fish on those lures, because they fish those lures more than any other lures. So, I believe in trying new lures, fishing them in way that's different from how anyone else is fishing them, and you may just catch more crappie than other anglers who use conventional tactics to catch fish.

Chapter 8 - What Tactics Pay-Off for Hot-Weather Crappie

Hot Weather Crankin' for Crappie with Kent Driscoll

Editor's Note: Kent Driscoll of Cordova, Tennessee, has fished for crappie for over 30 years and competes in national crappie tournaments each season.

Question: Kent, how do you catch crappie when the weather's almost too hot to breathe?

Driscoll: I'll troll crankbaits all summer, fishing for suspended crappie. Right now, the crappie are just starting to get into their summer pattern and following big schools of shad out on the flats. I start early in the morning pulling shallow-running crankbaits, like Bandit 200s and Strike King Series 3s. These crankbaits run about 8- to 11-feet deep. As the sun rises, the crappie go down a little deeper and move from 12- to 16-feet deep in the lakes I'll be fishing this summer. So, I'll switch over to the Bandit 300s and the Strike King Series 5 crankbaits. I'll use deep-diving crankbaits as the crappie move deeper because of the light penetration and the action from water skiers and jet skiers on the surface. The surface temperature's getting warmer also causes the crappie to move deeper.

Question: What color crankbaits will you be using in the hot summer months?

Driscoll: Early in the morning, I'll fish with darker colors, like solid black, black and plum and a lot of crawfish colors. I like matte-brown colors, too. A number of the crawfish colors have orange bellies, which the crappie seem to like. But with the clear water caused from the lack of rain in my area, when the sun rises, I'll switch to more-

82

natural colors. The Citrus shad, has recently been producing a number of crappie hot-pink and orange Crush colors have been productive on crappie.

Question: On what line will you be pulling these crankbaits?

Driscoll: I'll be using 12-pound-test line and pulling eight-different crankbaits at once. I'm casting the crankbaits out behind the boat and running long lines. Typically, I start at the back of the boat and use an 8-foot trolling rod with a Cabela's line-counter reel. That line will probably run out 120 feet. On the opposite side of the boat, I'll have the line out about 100 feet. On my next rod holder, I'll have a 10-foot rod and run that bait at 110 feet on one side and 90 feet on the other side of the boat. My third pole will be a 12-foot trolling rod. I'll have the line out 90 feet on one side of the boat and 80 feet, on the other rod on the other side of the boat. Then I'll use a 14-foot trolling rod. I'll have one line out at about 80 feet and on the other side of the boat I'll have my line out 70 feet.

I'm stair-stepping my baits. On one side of the boat I'll run my crankbaits more shallow than on the other side of the boat, until I learn at what depth the crappie are holding. Once I determine the depth where the most crappie are holding, I'll tighten my spread of baits and probably run them within 5 feet of each other. I never want to run my baits at the same lengths of line because all my lines will get tangled when I turn the boat. So, if I keep about 5 feet of separation on the amount of line I have out on each pole, I won't get tangled. By running poles of different lengths and lures at various depths, my lines won't get tangled-up when I catch a crappie that comes up behind the boat. The line that the crappie is on doesn't run into another line that may be more shallow. To effectively troll crankbaits, make sure you use different-length poles, and troll your crankbaits at various depths to keep your lines from tangling.

Question: How fast will you be trolling?

Driscoll: The ideal speed at which I'll troll is 1.5- to 1.7-miles per hour, and I'll determine that speed by using a GPS that can monitor speed down to 1/10 of a mile. Now, there are days when the crappie will take the bait better when it's pulled slower and other days when the crappie prefer the crankbaits pulled faster. That's one of the puzzles you'll have to put together to catch crappie in the summer, just like you'll have to determine what color of crankbait the crappie want each day you fish. On certain days, the crappie like some colors better than others. So, when I start fishing, I'll vary the colors of crankbaits I'll use, as well as the speed at which I'll troll. Too, I'll change the depths at which I'll troll. Then, as I begin to catch crappie, I usually can determine the depth where the crappie are feeding, the color of crankbait they prefer, and the speed at which the boat needs to travel for the crappie to take the bait the best. As I begin to put this pattern together, I'll change each component part – color, depth and speed – to make up the pattern to determine exactly what the crappie want on the day I'm fishing. On most days, I'll have one pole that catches the most crappie, which will indicate that this pole is either at the right depth or the color of lure on that pole is the one the crappie prefer on that day. Once I determine the color of lure the crappie want and the depth at which the crappie want to feed, I'll begin to adjust the speed of the boat. Using this system, I can maximize the number of crappie I'll catch each day.

Question: What size crappie will you catch in hot weather?

Driscoll: I'll be fishing Sardis, Enid, Arkabutla and Grenada lakes in Mississippi, and each of those lakes has a 12-inch minimum for the crappie you can keep. A 12-inch crappie on one of these lakes will weigh 1 pound. Right now, I'm catching about two throwbacks for every one crappie I keep. So, about two-thirds of the crappie I'll catch will be released because they'll be short. But I'll catch a lot of 13- and 14-inch crappie, and occasionally a 15-inch crappie. Trolling crankbaits gets more productive as the summer continues. The crappie are just starting to recuperate from the spawn and feeding heavily to put on weight. So, as the summer progresses, and we move into the fall, I'll start catching bigger crappie.

Question: Over what type of places will you be trolling in the late summer and early fall?

Driscoll: I'll start trolling on the big flats. The crappie pretty much school-up, feed and chase shad all night. Most of the time I'll find the crappie suspended out in the middle of the lake, holding on big flats. So, I'll be trolling in water 23- to 35-feet deep. If I don't locate the crappie on the flats, I'll start trolling the points. If they're not on the underwater points, then I'll troll the river channel or the secondary creek edges. But I'll catch most of my crappie at this time of year out on big flats in open water.

Summertime Crappie with Stokes McClellan by Fishing Deep and Using Your GPS

Editor's Note: The right water temperature and oxygen content are the keys to successfully finding crappie in July and August. Stokes McClellan of Huntersville, North Carolina, will tell us how to find and catch crappie during these months.

Question: Stokes, how will you catch crappie when the weather's really hot?

McClellan: I'll find most of my crappie in the mouths of feeder creeks close to the river channel. I also will locate crappie on underwater river ledges and underwater bends of the old river channel. In my area, we fish in water depths of 18 to 25 feet during the summer.

Question: Why will the crappie be holding in the mouths of feeder creeks?

McClellan: The bait's moving out of the creeks, and the shallow water in the creeks is starting to warm-up. So, the crappie move out toward the main part of the lake to hold on their summer pattern in deep water. Crappie also search for current or flow, which usually carries more-cool and more-oxygenated water than the main part of the river.

Question: Why will you be fishing the mouths of creeks in July and August?

McClellan: Most anglers miss good crappie fishing by not checking the mouths of creeks then. The water's generally deeper where the creek runs into the river channel, and if that creek is either spring-fed or running over rocks before it comes into the lake, it may be cooler or more oxygenated. Dissolved oxygen stays in cool water better than it does in hot water, and often the water temperature in the creek will be 2- to 4-degrees cooler than the temperature in the main river channel. You'll find crappie concentrating at the mouths of these creeks where the cool water meets the warm water. If you can locate a spring-fed creek coming into the river, you'll find crappie holding there. Besides attracting crappie, the right water temperature and dissolved oxygen also draw baitfish for the crappie to eat. Crappie will hold in the mouths of cool-water creeks all summer.

Question: How big of a temperature change do you want to see from the water in the river?

McClellan: If you can find as little as 2-degrees-cooler water in the creek than the temperature of the water at the same depth in the main river, the crappie will be holding in the creek mouths. Oftentimes we'll see as much as a 4-degree temperature change in these cool-water creeks.

Question: Why will the crappie be holding on main-river ledges?

McClellan: The ledges provide a place where crappie can move up and down in the water column without having to travel any distance. In the morning, when the water temperature's cool, the crappie can move-up and suspend in more-shallow water. The crappie usually will feed on tops of the ledges where the bait's easier to catch. Then as the sun rises, and the weather gets hotter, the crappie can sink down and hold above, beside or below the ledge. Crappie prefer to move vertically as the temperature changes, rather than horizontally.

Question: Will the crappie be suspended over the main-river channel?

McClellan: Most of the crappie are suspended, but they'll be suspended close to some type of bottom-contour change. They like either a bend in the river or a 20-foot ledge that drops off into the main-river channel. Too, I've noticed that if I can find the crappie holding close to the ledge, they're much easier to catch than if they're suspended above, below or off to the right or the left of the ledge.

Question: How will you catch these crappie?

McClellan: I'll fast-troll for the crappie using a heavier jig than I do in the spring. I'll use a 1/8-ounce jighead during the summer months as opposed to a 1/16- and a 1/32-ounce jig that I fish throughout most of the rest of the year. Not only do we use heavier jigheads, we also fish with bigger grubs like 3-inch ones during July and August. The shad are larger at this time of year, and the crappie are more aggressive. The crappie key-in on larger baits.

Question: What jigs do you use, and what color skirt seems to be the best?

McClellan: I prefer the Charlie Brewer Crappie Slider motor oil-colored jigs. The Culprit Tassel Tail Worms also are productive because they give a slightly-bigger image than the curly-tail worms. I also like Bass Pro Shops' Triple Ripple baits and the 9-foot B'n'M Sam Heaton Super-Sensitive rod. I also will use the 12-, the 14- and the 16-foot B'n'M trolling rods.

Question: Do you use a lead on the line to get those jigs down to that deeper water?

McClellan: No, I only use the weight of the jig. I make a long cast – about 80- to 90-feet away from the boat – and run my trolling motor or my big motor at 0.7 or 0.8 miles per hour. That gets my jig down to about 20 feet on 4-pound-test line. If I increase my speed to 1-mile per hour, my jigs will be running at 16- to 18-feet deep.

Question: During July and August, how many and what size crappie will you catch?

McClellan: In a day of fishing, I'll catch about 75 crappie and a number of these crappie will be in the 1-1/

2-pound class. We also catch plenty of small crappie, even on large baits.

Question: Why are most people not fishing deep water in the hot summer?

McClellan: Fishing this way may be a little-more difficult for people, because you have to really pay attention to your electronics to keep your boat right on the breakline. Using a GPS in conjunction with your depth finder can make a difference. When I see crappie on my depth finder, I'll mark those crappie as a waypoint on my GPS. Then I'll turn around and troll over them again. I've found that crappie don't tend to move as much in the hot-summer weather as they do at various times of the year. Therefore, if you find an area where you see a lot of crappie holding, you can fish that section all day. Too, I prefer to fish at this time of year because there's not nearly as much boat traffic, especially in the middle of the day, as there is in the spring and the fall. I've found that from daylight to about 10:30 am is when I catch the most crappie using this technique.

Question: What lakes do you fish at this time of year?

McClellan: I fish High Rock Lake and Lake Wylie in North Carolina.

Question: So, you believe there's still plenty of good crappie to be caught, even during the hottest part of the year, if anglers will fish deeper, use heavier jigs and pay attention to their depth finders?

McClellan: That's what I'll be doing.

Hair Jigs Tipped with Minnows Will Catch August Crappie with Roger Gant

Editor's Note: Roger Gant of Corinth, Mississippi, operator of Super Pro Guide Service on Pickwick Lake, which forms the boundaries of Alabama, Mississippi and Tennessee, has guided on Pickwick Lake for 25 years.

Question: Roger, most people seem to think crappie die in August, but that's not true, is it?

Gant: No, crappie don't die-off in August. They have to eat all year, and 1 or 2 weeks after the spawn's ended, they feed just as heavily as they do the rest of the year. In July and August, when the shad minnows get big enough to eat, the crappie start feeding on them. Summer is an excellent time to find and catch crappie, and July and August are great months for catching crappie.

Question: Where do you find crappie, and how do you catch them in August?

Gant: We generally catch August crappie by fishing hair jigs tipped with small minnows, but many anglers are now pulling crankbaits. However, I still prefer to fish with hair jigs tipped with minnows for my bait. I especially like to fish them with my Roger Gant Signature Series B'n'M Pole I helped design. I also like to fish the new Difference pole, which comes in two lengths – 8 and 9 feet.

Question: Roger, what makes the Difference a good pole?

Gant: When we're side-pulling for crappie, along with other techniques, we depend on the poles to tell us when we're getting a bite, which is what I call sight-fishing. We lay our poles down on the gunwale of the boat and watch the tips of our poles to see when the crappie take the jigs. You need an extremely-sensitive tip to see a crappie bite very-lightly on a jig trolled with the boat pulled sideways. The B'n'M Difference pole has a much-lighter tip than most poles, but it's not so light that it wilts or hangs down when you're fishing. I'll put two, 1/4-ounce jigs on the line. I don't want the weight of those jigs to pull my pole down. However, I want the pole to be sensitive enough that I practically can see a crappie breathe on my jig before the strike.

To have a super-sensitive tip, instead of only considering the sensitivity of the last 6 inches of the tip, the sensitivity in the tip of the pole needs to extend for at least 1 foot back. A specially-built rod or pole is hard to build that's sensitive enough to show the strike, but strong enough to keep the rod tip straight and not cause it to wilt. If the rod tip is so weak that it bends the tip when you're trolling the jigs, you can't see the strike as well as you can on a rod tip that holds the line straight out. By having the sensitivity run further down the rod, the strike's more well-defined. Then you can see the bite better, react better to the strike and catch more crappie than you miss. For me, a better pole makes the difference in how-many crappie you put in the boat on every trip.

I like the 9-foot rods to be on each end of the boat and turned away from the boat. This way, we get maximum coverage when we're side-pulling. In the middle of the boat, I prefer the 8-foot rods, because they're far enough from the sides of the boat to keep the jigs from getting tangled, but close enough for all the fishermen to see the bites on the ends of the poles. Certain lengths of rods give you more control over the fish than other lengths. For instance, an 8-foot rod gives you more control over the crappie than a 6-1/2-foot rod does. I've learned that you can control the fish better with an 8- or a 9-foot rod than you can with a 10- or a 12-foot rod. I'll have three people fishing from the boat when the boat's being pulled sideways. By having the 8-foot rods in front of the fishermen and the 9-foot rods on either end of the boat, the tips of the rods are close enough to see the strike, and the lengths of the rods are long enough to allow the fishermen to control the crappie they catch, without tangling the other fishermen's lines.

August Crappie Trolling with Billy Blakely

Editor's Note: Billy Blakely, the lodge manager and longtime guide at Blue Bank Resort on Reelfoot Lake near Tiptonville, Tennessee, has a job that requires him to find good fishing for his customers. Each day Blakely and his crew of guides have to stay in touch with where the crappie

are, and what they're doing and figure-out how to catch them.

Question: Billy, where are you finding and how are you catching crappie in August and early September?

Blakely: Right now our crappie at Reelfoot are holding in 8 feet of water over a 12-foot bottom. The fish are suspended, and I think they're holding on the thermocline.

Question: How are you catching them?

Blakely: We're putting out 12 and 14-foot trolling poles and slow-trolling over the stump beds, using the Capps & Coleman Minnow Rigs.

Question: How are you rigging?

Blakely: We're using 8-pound-test line and a 1/4-ounce lead on the minnow rigs.

Question: Why are you using B 'n' M Capps & Coleman Minnow Rigs?

Blakely: Reelfoot Lake was created because of an earthquake. The earthquake created a big gap in the ground, and all of the trees growing where that gap appeared fell into the lake. For this reason, Reelfoot is a really-stumpy lake and is loaded with underwater trees. If you try to spider-rig or slow-troll in Reelfoot, you will get hung-up. You may spend as much time trying to get your hooks out of underwater trees as you do trying to get your hooks out of crappie. However, we've learned with the Capps & Coleman Minnow Rigs that when one of our hooks catches on one of those underwater trees, all we have to do is take the pole out of the rod holder, back the pole up a few feet and shake the pole, and the weight that's above the last hook on the crappie rig will cause that crappie rig to come out of the wood. This is an extremely-efficient way to get your hooks and your crappie rigs back without having to break-off lines. By using this technique, we can continue to troll and catch more crappie. If you're going to troll (spider-rig) for crappie with minnows, and you're trolling over stumpy terrain, you'll really appreciate the Capps & Coleman Minnow Rigs, if you've never used them previously.

Question: What size minnows are you fishing now?

Blakely: I prefer the small minnows that are about 2-1/2-inches long. The shad that the crappie are feeding on now are about 2-inches long, so I want to give the crappie a minnow that's about the size of what they've been eating.

Question: What size crappie are you catching?

Blakely: Our crappie are weighing from 1/2- to 1-1/4-pounds here at the end of August. We can usually keep 40-75 in a morning of fishing in that range, and we generally throw back another 30 to 50 that are too small.

Question: How will you fish for crappie at Reelfoot once the weather starts cooling off in Late September?

Blakely: We'll fish with single poles like a 7-foot, 6-inch one, and I'll put a sliding bobber on it and fish with a jig. I'll pitch that jig and cork around visible stumps because our crappie will begin moving into the shallow water as the weather gets cooler. We usually see that crappie movement about the last week of September or the first week of October here at Reelfoot.

Shallow Crappie in August – Why and Where with the Jim Reedys

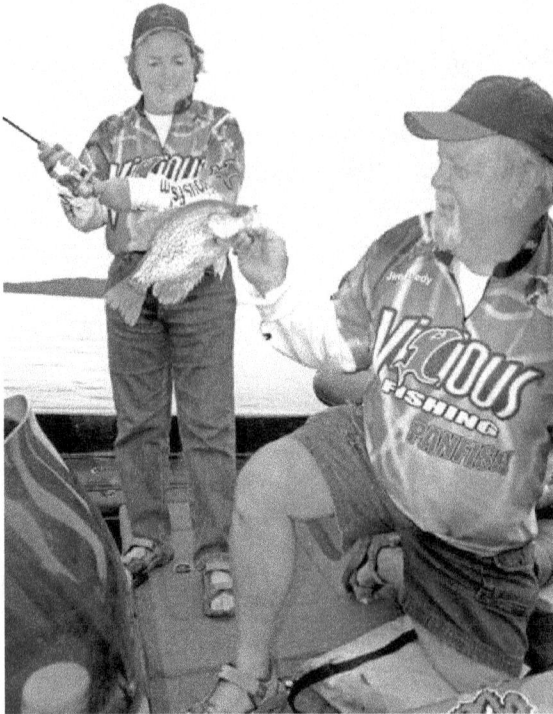

Editor's Note: Jim and Barbara Reedy, a husband-and-wife team from Charleston, Missouri, have tournament crappie fished for two decades. Their home lakes are Reelfoot and Kentucky lakes. These two crappie fishermen

also travel to about 20 tournaments each year all over the nation from Florida to Minnesota. "We like to travel the country, meet new people and learn a lot of new crappie techniques," Jim Reedy explains.

Question: Jim, at this time of the year, where are you finding crappie, and how are you catching them?

Jim Reedy: At this time of the year, the water across U. S. lakes is from warm to hot, and most fishermen think the crappie will be deep. We have found that the opposite is true. We'll often locate our crappie in 5 to 10 feet of water, or less. We're looking for big balls of schooling shad. Any place we can find the shad surfacing or running the banks, we'll generally pinpoint some crappie fairly close to those schools of shad. We may be fishing over 18 feet of water, but perhaps we'll be catching crappie at 7- or 8-foot deep. Sometimes we'll find the shad close to shore, and we may catch crappie in 5 to 6 feet of water. We'll slow-troll with 12-foot rods. We prefer the Capps & Coleman Double Minnow Rigs and usually fish with live minnows, although from time to time we will fish with jigs tipped with minnows. Our favorite color jig is blue and chartreuse.

Question: How many crappie do you usually catch when you're fishing in August?

Jim Reedy: We can usually catch a limit, but we'll only keep about 20. We don't fish to see how many crappie we can catch. We prefer to catch and keep just the big crappie.

Question: What's the biggest crappie you and Barb have ever caught?

Jim Reedy: Barb has caught a 4-pound crappie, and I've caught two or three 3-1/2-pound crappie, but I've never been able to break over into that 4-pound fish.

Question: What pound-test line are you using, Jim?

Jim Reedy: Barb and I prefer to fish with 6-pound-test high-vis line. Once in a while, we may fish 8-pound-test line, but we really prefer the 6-pound-test. We really prefer the high-vis line, because we can see the stripes on the line better, and we miss fewer fish with line than we do with line that's not Hi Vis. We usually troll with minnows, but if we do use jigs we'll tip the jig with either a minnow or a Berkley's Crappie Nibble.

Question: How are you keeping your minnows alive?

Jim Reedy: We use a Frabill Min-O Dipper Minnow Bucket with an aerator built into it. This bucket looks more like a cooler than it does a round minnow bucket. We've learned that if we pour cold water into that minnow bucket in the morning, the minnows will live all day long, if we keep the lid shut and the aerator running.

Question: How many minnows of what size will you and Barb usually take with you for a day of minnow fishing?

Jim Reedy: We usually buy a pound of minnows and put them in our Frabill minnow bucket. And although the minnows may look like they're crowded, they're really not. We may have to add a little ice to the water on really-hot days, but most of the time we don't have a problem with our minnows dying.

Question: With what size minnows do you like to fish?

Jim Reedy: We're firm believers in the old adage that big minnows produce big crappie. But if the weather gets really hot in the summertime often we feel we can catch more fish, if we downsize our minnows and fish with a somewhat smaller minnow than we usually do.

Question: Why do you think that the crappie are holding more shallow than most fishermen are fishing at this time of the year?

Jim Reedy: You have to remember that the crappie will follow the shad. If the shad are swimming near the surface, the crappie won't be far from them. If you're fishing along a creek channel that has a flat right beside it, the shad will often pull up out of that deep water and move up on that flat to feed. When they do, the crappie will be close behind them.

Question: Jim, at this time of the year, anglers will often see bass busting through the schools of shad on the surface. Will the crappie be holding near those schools just like the bass?

Jim Reedy: The crappie will usually be blowing-up on the surface eating shad like the bass do, but more than likely they'll be holding under that school of shad or just off to the side of the school of shad. I wear polarized sunglasses at this time of the year to see the shad under the water. If I can spot a big school of shad, I know the crappie will be related to that school somewhere. So, just because the temperature may climb to 100 degrees, don't assume that the crappie are 30-feet deep. They can be just as easily holding in 5 feet of water. Just remember, wherever you find the shad this month is where you'll find the crappie.

Crappie Fishing at Night When the Weather's Too Hot to Fish

From now until late September in the Deep South, the weather's just about too hot to fish. Yes, you can fish from daylight to about 10:00 am without getting fried like a red tomato, and you also can fish in the late afternoon from 4:00 pm until dark to avoid some of the heat. But the good news is, if you really want to do some serious fishing, night time is the right time to catch crappie all summer and in September.

If you go over almost any bridge during the summer months, when you reach the other side and look up under the bridge, there will appear to be firefly conventions, especially around the bridge pilings. The best bridge pilings to crappie fish are usually the bridge pilings sitting on the edges of creek channels. Those bridge pilings offer vertical structure for the crappie to hold on all the way from the very bottom of the channel up to the surface. By hanging a lantern or a light overboard or using a floating light, the light will attract baitfish, which will bring-in crappie moving up and down the channel. This is where most night crappie fishermen fish. If you want to avoid the crowd and not battle for the bridge papermouths, then use your lake maps and your GPS to locate underwater creek and river channels that intersect with the main river channel that also have brush and stumps on them.

Have you ever seen the cloverleaf designs of roads on major highways that can take motorists in four-different directions, depending on where they want to go, and how they want to get there? These highway cloverleafs funnel a lot of traffic in different directions the same way creeks that intersect the main river channel direct crappie moving

100

up and down the river and creek channels. Have you ever noticed the truck stops near the cloverleaf on the interstate where truckers from anywhere can stop and get a hot meal? That's what the brush piles and stake beds are like to the crappie that is moving up and down the creek and river channels. By anchoring your boat a pole's length from the brushpile on the shallow-water side of the creek or river channel and putting your lights out in the water, you often can catch crappie all night long. You may not get very many bites for the first half of the night, but between midnight and dawn, the crappie will swarm these spots. Use live minnows and a cork with your pole, and set-out several poles at different depths until you determine where the crappie is holding. The longer you fish, the higher up in the water the crappie will move. If you're looking for a way to bring home fillets for a Friday-night fish fry, then using your poles and fishing the intersections with brush on them where creek channels meet river channels is the most-productive way to catch a lot of crappie in the cool of a summer's evening.

Night fishing is a great family sport and a fun way to take your family fishing without having to fight the heat. You can use longer poles for this type of fishing. Light line and lively minnows will make your evening highly successful. You'll often catch catfish, white bass and an occasional hybrid striper or largemouth bass too, using this tactic.

Chapter 9 - How to Catch Sunburned Crappie

Tactics with Philip Criss and John E. Phillips

As sweat poured from my brow, I watched my quill sink. I set the hook and wrestled a fat slab crappie to the surface before putting my waiting dip net beneath the fish. The speckled side weighed 2-1/4-pounds – one of the many big crappie Philip Criss of McCalla,, Alabama, and I caught in air temperatures ranging from 90 to 105 degrees in the middle of the day as happens in August across the South in 4 to 8 feet of water.

Current Crappie

To catch hot-weather crappie, a fisherman must know what causes crappie to leave their deep-water haunts and move into shallow water when the temperature climbs high enough to fry eggs on the sidewalk. Crappie, basically slack-water feeders, will change their feeding patterns when a hydroelectric company pulls current through a lake. As the moving current causes the water's temperature to cool, baitfish will move to shallow water and feed along the edge of the current. The crappie will begin to feed actively on those baitfish.

"I look for shallow, underwater points where an old creek channel runs into the main river channel," Criss, an avid crappier, explains. The crappie holding in the creek and river channels will move to the up-current side of an underwater creek channel to hold in the slack water when current starts coming down the lake. When crappie want to feed, they move to the edge of the creek channel and attack the baitfish and shad that are holding on the edge barely off the current."

When I fished with Criss, we cast upstream using light spinning tackle, wire crappie hooks and small pieces of shot lead to sink the bait near the bottom. Every time our minnows got close to or passed over the lip of the underwater creek channel, the crappie would attack. If the cork didn't sink after it had floated 2- to 3-feet away from the lip of the break, we reeled-in our lines and cast up-current. When the fish quit biting around 1:00 pm, Criss suggested we try the blow-downs on the main river channel.

Shallow-Water Blow-Downs on the Main River Channel

Most bass fishermen fish trees that have blown-over into the water from the stumps of these trees down into the trunks and out over the limbs into deep water. I thought Criss and I would fish using this technique when he said we would fish some old blow-downs. We slowly motored up to a tree stuck in a mud flat in only about 2-1/2-feet of water. The roots of the tree pointed upstream, and half of the trunk and half of the top of the tree remained above the surface and pointing downstream. As we approached the tree, I told Criss, "I don't see enough water around that tree to float a crappie." Criss smiled mischievously and recommended that I leave my pole in the boat, and said, "Let me catch the fish." Criss dropped his minnow in the water up current of the roots. I watched as the bobber floated toward the roots, stopped and then sank. Criss muscled a 1-1/2-pound crappie away from the tree roots.

After watching Criss take the second fish, I flipped my bait upstream, let it wash toward the roots of the tree and started catching crappie, too. "The root ball of the tree not only stops the current when the water pulls through the lake, but it also creates a reverse current," Criss says. "Once the water hits the roots and changes direction to flow upstream, a dead spot forms just under the surface of the water. You'll find crappie holding in this slack water." I also learned that the force of the current coming downstream had dug the mud bottom away from much of the root system of the tree. By fishing immediately behind the root system, I discovered slack water containing plenty of big crappie. Anytime you can find a tree lying pointed upstream on a shallow flat with its roots exposed, you can assume you may find a deep hole in front of or behind the root system. Remember, the tree breaks the current and creates a cool, well-oxygenated and bait-rich slack-water area when the current runs. However, you won't find this spot nearly as productive when the current doesn't run.

Deep-Water Blow-Downs on the Main River

At our third fishing spot during a day of hot-weather crappie hunting, Criss and I moved to a tree that recently had fallen in the water on the edge of a steep bluff. Criss explained to me that crappie would hold in this area because they'd have shallow-water cover that broke the current and concentrated baitfish on the edge of a deep-water drop. "Any place you can find a current break in shallow water on the main river channel that can hold baitfish, you'll find an ideal hot-weather crappie spot," Criss reports. "One of the real problems is that in many lakes during the heat of the summer a current doesn't come through the lake until later in the morning when the weather is too hot for most anglers to fish. I like to fish at that time of day because I won't see other fishermen on the lake watching me catch crappie and then later stealing my fishing spots."

Most anglers, excluding Criss, believe you can't catch crappie from 10:00 a.m. to 3:00 p.m. during the hot summer months when the temperature climbs over 90 degrees. Therefore Criss chooses the midday as his favorite time to crappie fish and you can too.

Highway to Hot-Time Crappie

Larry Bettison of Georgetown, Georgia, a sneaky, hot-weather crappie fishermen, rarely if ever lifts the lid on his ice chest or his live well when someone asks, "Have you caught any fish?" Rather than lie, Bettison just wipes his brow and says, "The weather's so hot out on the lake, I can't believe a fish will bite anywhere." But Bettison grins on the inside after his comment. He knows he has a cooler full of big slab crappie he's caught at a time when and a place where most other anglers don't fish during the summer months.

"Lake Eufaula in Eufaula, Alabama, near my home, has three or four underwater bridges that are still intact," Bettison explains. "You can find these bridges by looking at old road and river maps that show train trestles and bridges crossing small creeks and rivers before the lake was impounded. Crappie often will suspend under these bridges and above these old creek channels. But even if you know crappie are holding around underwater bridges, you'll have difficulty catching them, unless you use two grappling hooks."

Bettison tried to catch the underwater-bridge crappie for several years before he developed his grappling-hook technique. One bridge he fished lay out on the main part of the lake where waves caused his anchors to come up and moved his boat away from the edge of the bridge. "I learned that if my minnows or jigs didn't fall right beside the bridge where the crappie could see them, the fish wouldn't move out from under the bridge to attack my baits," Bettison reports. "If I anchored on top of the bridge and tried to fish the edge of the bridge, when the waves hit the boat and the boat rocked, the anchors would come up off the top of the bridge and move my boat away from the edge of the underwater bridge. I couldn't find a way to keep my line lying right along the edge of the underwater bridge so my minnow would put on a show for the crappie under the bridge."

Not one to accept defeat, Bettison came up with a grappling-hook tactic that would allow his boat to stay right on the lip of the break and let him fish with his line lying right beside and touching the old bridge. "I made an anchor resembling a grappling hook from pieces of aluminum with a 4-foot piece of aluminum sticking straight up and four spikes coming off of the main shaft," Bettison said. "I'd lower the grappling hook and catch the underside of the bridge with at least two of the four prongs. Then I'd tighten up on the rope and run the end of the rope through a bungee cord I'd hooked onto the cleat on the side of my boat. Once I got the first grappling hook secured to the side of the bridge, I'd hook up a second grappling hook to the stern. The grappling hook would hold the boat next to the bridge. The bungee cord let the boat rock back and forth without creating slack on the rope that held the grappling hook to the base of the bridge. Next, I baited my rods with live minnows and slowly let the lines down the side of the bridge. I kept most of my rods lying inside the boat with just the tips of the rods over the side of the boat. I usually could feel the side of the bridge with my line as I lowered a minnow down so it could swim right on the bottom edge of the bridge where the crappie were holding. The bridge provided shade, structure and a place for the baitfish to concentrate."

Although a number of people fish the bridge, Bettison has learned to fish a more-specific, productive places. Bettison fishes the edges of two pilings that sit on the underwater riverbank and support the span of the bridge. "Those bridge pilings offer vertical structure over the edge of the deep water, which means the crappie can hold vertically wherever they want under the shade of the bridge," Bettison said. Often at night during the summer months, Bettison will use his grappling hooks to hold him on the break of the old underwater bridge. He finds that crappie move out from under the bridge and hold on top of the bridge when the sun goes in and the moon comes out. "The later I fish into the night, the closer to the surface I'll catch crappie," Bettison advised. "The fish will move up because I use either a Coleman lantern or floating lights to attract the baitfish on which the crappie will feed." With Bettison's grappling-hook method, he holds his boat on the lip of the break. He can fish the minnow either under the submerged bridge by day or on top of the bridge by night.

Doughnut-Hole Crappie

Dr. Omar Smith of Memphis, Tennessee, taught me how to fish doughnut-shaped root systems in shallow ponds and oxbow lakes off main river systems for crappie when the temperature sizzles. "In the centers of some oxbow lakes, I'll fish live cypress trees, which provide shade and cover in two different places," Smith says. "Obviously, shade will appear first around a cypress tree at the trunk. You'll find crappie holding in that shade and relating to the trunk of the tree." But if Smith doesn't catch any crappie holding around the trunk, he's not stumped. Because Smith knows the way a cypress tree grows, he realizes a doughnut-shaped root system starts from the stump of the tree below the water and spreads out 3- to 4-feet away from the tree's trunk. "If the crappie don't hold close to the trunk, then I fish 3- to 4-feet away from the trunk on either side of the doughnut-shaped root system," Smith reported. "I think that fishing in the middle of the day gives me an advantage. With the sun straight overhead, most of the shade from the tree will be right under the tree at the trunk or immediately under the root system all the way around the tree. "Then when the sun rises or sets, the shade shifts to either side of a tree, which allows the crappie to hold in the shade away from the tree. That's why I catch most of my fish and particularly the biggest crappie in the middle of the day."

Smith quickly added that other factors such as the barometric pressure and the amount of wind on a lake on the day he fishes influence the success of his crappie fishing in the hot summer months. Smith also relies on the moon phase at any time of the year he fishes to determine whether or not he'll catch crappie. "I've found crappie bite better during the week of the full moon," Smith emphasized. "I believe when the sun and the moon are in equal proportions to each other or close to equal proportions to each other that fish, animals and even people feel much more comfortable and tend to move and feed better. I've also found the most productive fishing is two to three days before or after a full moon. When a full moon is shining, I believe the sun and the moon exert less pressure on the earth. Then the fish tend to bite better."

Another factor Smith has observed about crappie is the times of day the fish bite better under full-moon conditions. During a full moon, Smith has learned that crappie tend to bite better between 10:00 am and noon than they do early in the morning. "Perhaps fish bite better during these hours because they feed more actively at night during a full moon than they will under a dark sky," Smith suggested. Armed with this knowledge and realizing crappie tend to concentrate under trees in oxbow lakes in the middle of the day to find both shade and cover, Smith has deduced that on the morning after a full moon, the fish will feed between10:00 am and noon. In the summertime when the sun sizzles, the fish must concentrate under the trees standing out in theater. Therefore, you'll find the most productive way to catch crappie in the summertime in oxbow lakes is to fish on the morning after a full moon between 10:00 a.m. and noon under the trees.

To catch crappie, Smith prefers to fish with a jig pole and a 1/16- or a 1/32-ounce jig head. He likes either an 8-foot or a 10-foot graphite jig pole, because of its light weight. Six-pound-test clear line performs best in the shallow water because Smith believes crappie can see the line. If the crappie bite very slowly, Smith will lip-hook a live crappie minnow behind the skirt of his jig. He fishes with a tight line and moves his bait first around the trunk of the tree and then around the doughnut-shaped root system along the outer edge of the tree. When the spawn ends, and all the crappie have left the banks, you don't have to lay down your crappie poles and ultra light rods and start to fish for catfish. By using these tactics, you can continue to catch big, fat, slab-sized crappie – even when the weather sizzles.

Weather So Hot You Can Fry Eggs on the Sidewalk But You Still Can Catch Crappie

Editor's Note: Hot weather and clear water are most crappie fishermen's worst nightmares. But Ronnie Capps from Tiptonville, Tennessee, a co-winner of more than $1.5 million earned catching crappie, can catch crappie when the weather's so hot you can fry eggs on the sidewalk.

111

Question: Ronnie, you and your partner, Steve Coleman, have to fish hot weather at crappie tournaments. When you're fishing in June and July, how deep will the crappie be concentrated, and how will you catch them in that deep water?

Capps: The deepest I've ever caught crappie was on J. Percy Priest Lake, an impoundment on the Stones River in north-central Tennessee near Nashville, when I caught crappie in 65 feet of water. That's the first time I've deep-sea fished in fresh water. My partner Steve Coleman and I were fishing a tournament there a few years ago. We found some cedar bushes along the old river channel that were standing beside the Stones River before the reservoir was flooded. Those old cedar trees lined the entire river channel. We started fishing the biggest bushes we could find and used our bulldozer tactic to smash live minnows into those cedar trees. Steve and I only fished two poles each, but we finished third in the tournament.

You have to remember that when you're fishing a clear lake, you'll find crappie holding in the really-deep structures. Now, this only happens on lakes with current coming through them and enough oxygen for the crappie to survive in that deep water. Many lakes, however, stratify in the hot weather, and there's a thermocline at a certain depth where the water's cool but still oxygenated. Below that thermocline, there won't be enough oxygen for the crappie, or the water will be too cold to make the crappie comfortable. The lakes usually stratify and create a thermocline in July and August. You won't find current flowing in lakes like Reelfoot Lake or the Big Sandy South Arm on Kentucky Lake, and these lakes will form thermoclines when the weather gets hot. When a lake stratifies, a thermocline is created. The crappie will come-up out of that deep brush and suspend right along the edge of that thermocline. Before the hot weather, the crappie may have been holding tight (jammed) into that deep brush. However, when the thermocline starts to be created, and the oxygen level gets low in that deep water, the crappie and the baitfish will move-up and suspend along the thermocline. That's where the water is the most comfortable, and the crappie will have the oxygen the need to survive. When this occurs in the hot summer months, you really can catch a lot of crappie using crankbaits and the Capps and Coleman Crankbait Rigs.

Question: Do you ever pull crankbaits?

Capps: Yes, I do. I push them on the front of the boat and pull them on the back of the boat.

Question: Which poles do you use when you're pushing and pulling crankbaits?

Capps: I'll use the 14-foot trolling pole. On the poles I'm pushing, I'll often use a bell sinker as heavy as 4 ounces, depending on the water depth I'm fishing. When I'm pulling the crankbaits, I'll only use a 1-ounce sinker. B 'n' M has a Capps and Coleman Double-Crankbait Rig that allows Ronnie and I to pull and push two crankbaits on one pole. I'll generally push four poles off the front and pull two to four poles on the back of the boat. Steve's actually fishing on the front of the boat when we're trolling crankbaits, and I generally fish on the back of the boat.

Question: Over what types of areas do you troll crankbaits?

Capps: We try to follow underwater contours of creek channels, river channels, ditches and ledges. I try to keep my baits where there's the most structure any time of the year. Creek channels and river channels generally have a lot of structure on them. During the hot summer months, the crappie often will be suspended above those stumps. So, by following those creek channels and pushing and pulling crankbaits, you can have a fun day of fishing for and catching crappie, even on the hottest days of summer.

Question: Ronnie, why do you like a trolling pole when you're fishing your Double-Crankbait Rig?

Capps: I like a really-stiff pole that's much heavier, if you'll be pulling or pushing a 4-ounce bait, you need a stiffer pole to support the weight. When you're trolling for crappie, you want your pole to keep its shape as much as possible. To set the hook when you're trolling crankbaits, you need a firm pole.

Question: Ronnie, what crankbaits do you use?

Capps: I prefer the Rapala broken-back-designed crankbaits and the Bandit 300 Series crankbaits for the bottom lure.

Question: How does the Capps and Coleman Crankbait Rig differ from the Capps and Coleman Minnow Rig?

Capps: The crankbait rig has the lead on the bottom, instead of in the middle of the rig. But the Bandit 300 Series crankbait is on a 3-inch leader, so it's digging down below the lead.

Question: How's the rig set-up?

Capps: We have a three-way swivel with a bell sinker attached almost to the swivel, maybe 1/2- to 2-inches off the swivel. The other end of the swivel has 30 -inches of leader with a Bandit 300 Series crankbait attached to it. The last eye of the swivel is tied to my main line, which is 15-pound-test P-Line. When I put this rig in the water, the broken-back crankbait swims straight, and the Bandit 300 Series digs toward the bottom below the sinker. Using this rig, I can cover 6 feet of water when I'm trolling down these creek and river channels.

Question: What color crankbaits do you have tied-on, Ronnie?

Capps: They'll either be white or shad patterned, and I'll occasionally use the fire-tiger color. But white has always been my favorite. Using this tactic and these crankbaits, you can catch crappie even into August.

Brad Whitehead Explains How to Catch Crappie in Late August and Early September

Editor's Note: Brad Whitehead, from Muscle Shoals, Alabama, guides on Pickwick, Wilson and the Bear Creek lakes in north Alabama.

Question: Brad, where do you find crappie in late August?

Whitehead: We begin in the mornings trolling in 16-foot-deep waters. By the middle of the day, we're usually fishing in 24 feet of water.

Question: How do you get your bait down to crappie that deep?

Whitehead: I use two tactics. I use crankbaits trolled from the back of the boat. My number-two tactic is spider rigging.

Question: How do you get your crankbaits down to deep-water depths?

Whitehead: I'll put a 1/2- or 1-ounce egg-shaped leader up the line about 4 feet from my crankbait. Next, I'll loop my line through the egg sinker three times to have about 4 feet of line coming away from the sinker. Then, I'll tie my crankbait to the sinker. When I'm fishing without a weight, early in the mornings, I'll pull the crankbait with a 6.5-foot crappie spinning rod. For the other method, I'll use a 5-ounce weight up the line with two Mister Mino jig heads tied below the weight on a 7-1/2-feet-long rod.

Question: Brad, what kinds of areas are you trolling over?

Whitehead: I'll often change the regions I'll troll over from day to day. The biggest secret to catching crappie using this method is covering a lot of water. I'll troll flats to the edges of creek channels. At this time of year, I'll start in the mouths of creeks and troll about halfway to the back of the creeks. The creeks I'm trolling are big creeks that bring major amounts of water into the lakes. In the mornings while the light is still low, I'll start trolling the flat in 14 to 16 feet of water. I'll troll as shallow as 12 feet, if the water's cloudy. From 11 am to 1 pm, I'll move out to the main creek channel where I'll drop my leads all the way to the bottom, reel two or three times up from the bottom and begin trolling. When I'm trolling a creek channel, I'll have my crankbait running at 12 to 14 feet with my downriggers on the line just off the bottom. Some days I'll catch more on downriggers, and on other days I'll catch more on crankbaits. I'll keep downriggers and crankbaits on the flats, and I'll keep both just off the lips of the breaks. I'll troll with 16 poles and have 8 poles on the front of the boat and 8 poles on the back of the boat.

Question: What size crappie are you catching at this time of year, Brad?

Whitehead: They will be from 10- to 14-inches long. You can catch some really-nice crappie in late August and September. During August and early September, most crappie fishermen aren't fishing because they believe crappie don't bite then. But, often I'll catch bigger crappie in the hot part of August and September than I'll catch in the spring.

Question: Why do you like the Mister Twister Mister Mino at this time of year?

Whitehead: The Mister Mino is a little bigger than your normal crappie grubs. And, in August, I believe that the shad the crappie are feeding on are a little bigger than most crappie jigs. If you look at a Mister Mino, it's somewhat fatter than a 3-inch crappie grub. In August, I'll fish a white or white/chartreuse color combination.

Question: How many crappie do you usually bring in for a day of trolling?

Whitehead: We usually come in with 25 to 40 crappie in our ice chest after a half-day trip. We'll throw back at least that many. In late August and early September, the number of crappie you bring in varies quite a bit. Some years ago one week I had a 40-crappie day, and the week before that I brought in 27 per day. My average is in this range, but my numbers depend on how the crappie are biting, and what size crappie my clients want to catch. With 16 poles out, I can cover quite a bit of water and find good numbers of fish.

Question: Brad, why are you vertical jigging in September?

Whitehead: I like to vertical jig in the warm months like September to fish the stake beds I put out. Fishing this way also lets me practice finding the fish and catching them with a handheld pole in deep water. In the middle of the day, when the crappie move into deep structure and are holding tight, you can pick them out of that structure using a pole and a 1/16-ounce jig.

Question: Brad, what rod, reel and line are you using for vertical jigging?

Whitehead: I like the Buck's Ultimate 10-foot Rod with a reel on 8-pound-test line.

Question: Why do you like a 10-foot rod for vertical jigging in August?

Whitehead: With the 10-foot rod, I don't have to sit right on top of the crappie to catch them. I can stay at least 10-feet away from the structure and fish all the way around it without being right on top of the crappie. Using the 10-foot pole, I can fish all the way around structure, and the crappie will never know I'm there. Sometimes the crappie won't be right on top of this structure but may be off to the side or above the structure. So, if you get your boat right over the top of a piece of structure, the crappie may be holding behind you or directly under you. I like to stay away from the crappie with a longer pole. This way, I'll have a little more room to fish, and I can fish the structure more thoroughly. If you have a short pole, you'll have to hold your boat just above the structure.

Question: When you're vertical jigging, how deep is the water you're fishing?

Whitehead: The water is rarely deeper than 20 feet. I've found that you can't vertical jig effectively in water much deeper than 20 feet.

Question: What size jig are you using?

Whitehead: I like to use a 1/4-ounce jighead with a Mister Mino. Silver flake and black/chartreuse are the best colors.

Question: How do you know there are fish on the stake beds you're fishing?

Whitehead: I'll see the crappie on my depth finder before I start fishing a piece of structure. I can tell by the relationship of the crappie to the cover, whether or not the fish will bite. For instance, if the crappie are holding tight to the cover or are down in the cover, they're more likely to bite, than if they're on the sides of the cover. When I bang my jig into the cover, and fish are holding tight to it, I get more bites than when the jig falls, and the crappie takes the bait on the fall.

Question: How do you keep your jig from getting hung in the wood?

Whitehead: The stake beds I build will only have about eight stakes sticking up off the bottom. I've found that fishing a stake bed is easier, and you hang-up less often than you will fishing a brush pile made of treetop. I've found the smaller my stake beds, the bigger the crappie I'll catch on these stake beds. I have a stake-bed frame that builds beds 24-inches long and 24-inches wide, and I build them eight stakes high.

Question: In a day of fishing stake beds, how many crappie do you usually catch?

Whitehead: Because I'm fishing vertically, and I'm not covering as much water as I do when I'm spider rigging, a good day of fishing stake beds will produce 20 to 30 crappie. However, the crappie I catch off the stake beds are slightly bigger than the crappie I'll catch trolling. Often, I'll catch 13- to 15-inch crappie on my stake beds in September.

Chapter 10 - How to Catch Dog-Day Crappie with Roger Gant

Editor's Note: Roger Gant of Corinth, Mississippi, has fished Pickwick Lake on the Tennessee River for more than 40 years. Gant guides on Pickwick more than 200 days a

123

year and consistently catches limits of slab-sized crappie. Most crappie fishermen don't catch large numbers of fish during the "Dog Days" of summer, but Gant does.

"When the weather's really hot, I fish for crappie around an area with the largest amount of submerged wood I can locate," Gant says. "Pickwick Lake, where the barge traffic and the current help oxygenate the water, doesn't have a well-defined thermocline. For this reason, crappie will hold between 15- and 25-feet deep in warm temperatures, especially during July, August and the first half of September." To reel in Dog-Day crappie, Gant prefers to fish with 8-pound-test line and a 1/4-ounce hair jig. "A 1/4-ounce jig is more effective in hot weather than a 1/16-ounce jig because the weight of the 1/4-ounce jig will put it in deep water, and it will stay there when you troll with it," Gant comments. "At the depths that I fish, the water is dark, and the crappie can't decide the actual size of the jigs. They just attack the baits because they easily can detect the movements of those heavier jigs. Four-pound-test line probably will get more bites than 8-pound line will. But, I like to fish with 8-pound-test line, because I often catch crappie that weigh more than 2 pounds, and the 8-pound line holds the bigger crappie better than the smaller line does."

When the temperature climbs above 70 degrees, Gant tips his jigs with minnows. "I'll hook a live minnow from the top of its head just behind its brain to the jig," Gant explains. "By hooking the bait in this manner, the minnow stays on the hook longer than if I lip-hook it. Also, the crappie can hit the minnow several times without knocking the bait off the hook. Hooking crappie without tipping your jig may be easier. But, if I don't use a minnow in the summertime, I won't get many bites. Also, I'll catch two to three times more crappie fishing a jig with a minnow than I will fishing a jig without one." In addition to hooking live minnows to his jigs, Gant uses fish attractant on his jigs to entice hot-weather crappie. "I know from experience that I can catch more crappie on scented jigs than I can on unscented jigs," Gant remarks. "Fish attractant not only attracts crappie, it kills the human odor on the jigs. I once put fish attractant on a piece of cloth, hooked that cloth to a bream hook and caught several bluegills. The scent alone attracted the fish to that cloth."

How to Side-Pull for Dog Day Crappie

Gant doesn't use traditional trolling methods to catch crappie in the summertime; instead he side pulls. Gant places his trolling motor on the side of his boat instead of the back of the boat, which pulls his boat sideways. This side-pulling technique allows the anglers on Gant's boat to fish two rods each out one side of the boat and watch the lines and the rod tips for the slightest movements that may indicate strikes. "I'll move my boat sideways as slowly as possible in hot weather because I've discovered that summertime trolling is similar to wintertime trolling," Gant emphasizes. "Crappie prefer slower-moving baits during the summer and winter than they do in the fall or the spring when they feed more actively. Too, crappie become much more finicky in the summertime and often won't bite at all. The slower your boat moves when the fish are in a finicky mood, the more crappie you'll catch."

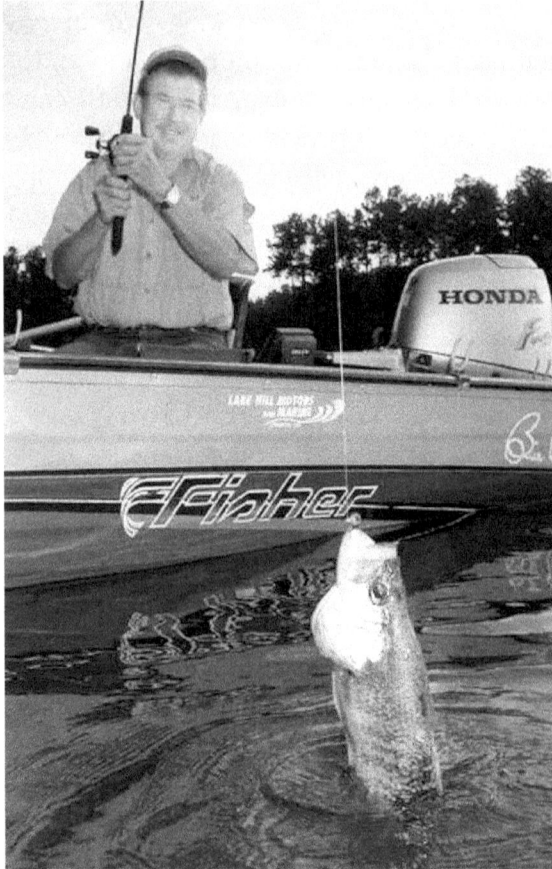

How, When and Why to Change Water Depths

The weather changes very little during the hottest part of the year. In July, August and September - and often into October - the weather conditions remain very stable. In the fall, spring and winter, however, the weather and the water conditions constantly change. Then Gant continuously must move his boat to different areas and water depths to find crappie. "I depend on my depth finder to search for large areas of brush in the middle of the lake," Gant states. "I know that I'll find the most crappie during the summer in the middle of the lake around wood structure. I also look for sections of a lake that have a lot of brush at different water depths because I know I'll have to change depths throughout the day to find actively-feeding crappie. I don't believe that crappie move to different depths throughout the day like some fishermen think. I'm convinced that the crappie that hold at various depths in the water will bite at different times. For example, in the middle of the day, the fish that hold in deep water seem to bite more. In the morning and the late afternoon, the crappie that are holding in the more-shallow water seem to bite best. During the summer, I'll start out fishing in 14-foot-deep water because the shallow-water crappie usually will bite first. By noon, I'll fish as deep as 18 feet. By 2:00 pm, I'll probably fish 22-feet deep. And, as the weather cools down in the afternoon, I'll start fishing shallow again."

How to Set Your Hook

"As deep as we fish in the summertime, you can set your hook fairly hard on crappie, because much of the force you put in the hook set dissipates in the amount of line between you and the crappie," Gant explains. "If you fish in the more-shallow water, and you make a hard hook set, you'll tear the hook out of the crappie's mouth. But, the techniques we use and the limber rods we fish with enable my fishermen to set their hooks fairly hard. Once you make a hook set, you must keep a bow in your rod to create tension on the line and keep the hook firmly planted in the crappie's mouth. If you have any slack in your line, the crappie can shake its head and force the jig out of its mouth. Just remember that crappie become more active at the surface in warmer water, and if any slack gets in your line, you easily can lose them. Also remember that in hot weather crappie often behave like children who don't want to eat. A child who doesn't want to eat will take his fork and push the food around on his plate, but he won't put the food in his mouth. Crappie don't have hands, so they can't move the bait around and decide if they want to eat. But, a crappie can put its mouth on the bait to test it out before it eats."

When crappie don't want to bite, Gant moves to the thickest underwater cover he can find. Then he tells his clients that they'll have to force-feed the crappie. "When force-feeding, I tell my clients to set the hook on the second bite instead of setting the hook as soon as we see the crappie bite," Gant says. "The rod tip will jump when a crappie bites the first time, but I won't do anything. The first time a crappie bites, it will hit the tail end of the bait. The second time it bites, the fish will take the bait deeper in its mouth to get a better feel. When I see the rod tip twitch the second time, I'll immediately set the hook. Using this technique, I'll usually catch more crappie - especially when the fish aren't in the mood to feed."

What Are Roger Gant's Top-10 Secrets for Dog-Day Crappie

Although Gant has special tactics for catching Dog Day crappie, he employs many of these same philosophies and equipment to take crappie at any time of the year.

1. Use the proper equipment. "Many crappie fishermen don't use the best equipment for the time of year they plan to fish," Gant says. "For

instance, if you use too large a line, your jig will float too high in the water for crappie to take it. If your line doesn't have the strength you need, you'll break the line when you set the hook. I've found that I can set the hook hard on 8-pound-test line, yet the small line will cut through the water so that my jigs run at the proper depths. A crappie fisherman also needs an extremely-soft rod with enough backbone to hold itself upright. I fish with a 6-1/2-foot crappie jig pole. I must have a sensitive rod, so that I can spot even the lightest crappie bite. Another important piece of equipment is your reel. I fish with bait-casting reels. I also prefer to use casting reels so I can count my line down to the proper water depth to catch the crappie. I put a white piece of tape on my rod 1 foot from where the line comes out of the reel. Then a fisherman can pull the line off the reel out to where the line crosses the white tape. Each time an angler pulls the line to the white tape, he knows his jig will go down one more foot in the water. By having the jigs troll at exactly the water depth where the crappie hold - or slightly above the crappie - we can catch more fish."

2. Fish the depths where crappie hold. "By constantly watching your depth finder and searching for fish and structure, you'll know at what depth you need to troll your jigs," Gant reports. "Then I can tell my fishermen how much line to pull off so the jigs will pass slightly above the depth where the crappie are holding."

3. Know where crappie hold in the lakes you plan to fish at the time of year you will fish for them. "Though many fishermen attempt to catch crappie

next to structure near the bank, I like to fish out in the middle of the lake year-round," Gant comments. "There's as much structure in the middle of the lake as there is on the bank. But, the crappie in the middle of the lake experience less fishing pressure than the crappie on the bank do. So, the crappie in the middle of the lake often bite better. Crappie will hold in different places at various times of the year under specific weather and water conditions. By using your depth finder to locate a number of spots in the lake where crappie hold during each season of the year, you can pattern crappie and always know their locations. For instance, to catch crappie in the summer, you must pinpoint areas with heavy structure where you can fish, regardless of the wind. Also, use your depth finder to locate crappie during the three distinct times of the day. If you fish in the summer, you need to find areas with heavy cover in 12 to 14 feet of water where you can fish in the early morning. Next, look for places in 14 to 16 feet of water that you can fish in the mid-morning. Then, search for spots with heavy structure in 18 to 22 feet of water to fish in the middle of the day."

4. Remember that crappie holding in different water depths will bite at various times of the day. "I don't believe that crappie move very much," Gant reports. "For example, if you catch crappie for the first two hours after daylight, and those crappie stop biting, the crappie haven't moved to deeper water. I think those crappie have stopped feeding in that spot. For instance, after working outside all day, you may go inside your house and eat

large amounts of food. But, you'll slow down your eating as you begin to get full. Then you won't eat again for awhile, regardless of how much food someone brings to the table. I believe crappie act the same way. To continue to catch fish after they stop biting, go to another spot that has similar structure at a deeper water depth. After 1:00 or 2:00 pm when you've caught the deepest-water crappie, fish for crappie in more-shallow water again."

5. Realize that the speed of your jig determines crappie-fishing success. "If crappie bite aggressively, troll the jigs at a faster speed," Gant recommends. "If the crappie act finicky or are not biting aggressively, then slow down the speed at which you troll but maintain the same water depth where you're trolling your jigs. The trolling speed often determines the number of crappie you'll catch in a day of fishing."

6. Tie two different-colored jigs on the same line when you troll. "Don't fish with two jigs of the same color on one line," Gant mentions. "Crappie don't care about the colors of the jigs. They can't distinguish between green, pink or orange jigs. But, under certain water and weather conditions, the crappie will be able to detect one of those colors better than the other colors. Fish usually will bite the colors they can see the best. For instance, the crappie in Pickwick Lake take chartreuse and lime-colored jigs best. However, if you move west of Pickwick Lake into Mississippi where the water becomes more stained, the crappie seem to prefer orange and pink colors. The soil in those lakes enables the fish to see

133

those colors better than chartreuse and lime. You'll have to learn which color of jigs the crappie will bite best where you fish."

7. Learn to read a depth finder. "A depth finder confirms the location of crappie, which means I can fish a spot with more confidence," Gant explains. "The depth finder also tells me how the crappie are relating to the structure. If the crappie are holding above the structure, I know how deep to let my jigs down so the fish will take them. If the crappie are holding in the structure, I know that I'll have to troll slower and let the jigs pass just barely above the structure to catch the crappie."

8. Use fish attractant to cover human scent. "Many fish attractants contain oil of anise, which can and will cause fish to bite," Gant says. "So, I use fish attractant on all my jigs. I don't know whether or not crappie can smell human odor as effectively as white-tailed deer can, but I do know that I catch more fish when the crappie can't smell me."

9. Put your rod tip in the water. According to Gant, "Anytime you set your hook on a crappie, you'll tear its mouth. Also, when the water temperatures increase in the summer, the crappie become much more active at the surface after they're hooked. Then they're much more likely to shake their heads and throw the jigs. If they get their heads out of the water, they can throw the hooks easier. By putting your rod tip under the water when the fish comes to the surface, you'll keep the crappie's head in the water, and it will be less likely to shake the jig out of its mouth."

10. Use a rubber dip net. "Jigs don't get caught in a rubber dip net as easily as they do in the basket of a dip net made from plastic or braided line," Gant mentions. "If you don't want to waste a third of your day untangling jigs, purchase and use a dip net with a rubber basket."

Chapter 11 - How to Locate Crappie

Fishing a New Lake

Editor's Note: Stokes McClellan of Huntersville, North Carolina, a crappie-fishing pro, travels the nation finding

136

and catching monster crappie. When there's money on the line, you can bet on Stokes McClellan. This week, we'll look at how McClellan finds crappie and what he does to make them bite.

Question: Stokes, what crappie circuits do you fish?

McClellan: I fish the Southern Crappie Association, the Crappie Masters and the Crappie USA tournaments.

Question: How many tournaments do you fish in a year?

McClellan: My partner (my son Adam) and I generally fish about 14 or so, and we usually can make enough money to pay all our expenses and finish the season with about $500 in our pockets. In our best year, we earned about $18,000 in tournament fishing. No one really gets rich fishing crappie tournaments, but if you love to compete, enjoy catching and eating crappie and really want to learn all you can about the sport, then you should fish crappie tournaments.

Question: Stokes, how do you find crappie when you fish a new lake?

McClellan: First, Adam and I buy a topographical map of the lake. From the topo map, we can see where the creek channels and the drop-offs are located, and where rivers and creeks enter the lake. We use this information to develop a game plan about where we should try to find crappie on the lake, why the crappie should be there, and in what part of the lake we'll spend most of our practice time. On most new lakes we fish, we'll usually try to fish the upper third of the lake. The upper third of the lake always seems to be the most-fertile section of a lake, and the point where the most nutrients enter the lake. In this section of the lake, you'll find better concentrations of baitfish and crappie.

Once we arrive at the lake and put our boat in the water, we'll travel to the spots we've noted on our topo map and look for bait and crappie. We're searching for crappie, of course, but because we're open-water trollers with our Poles, we're also trying to identify at what depth the baitfish are holding, and in what type of structure they're holding. A classic example will be a creek channel with plenty of stumps and brush in it that runs from 1- to 1-1/2-miles long. Along that edge, we'll want to see schools of baitfish. We know that if the baitfish are there, they're related to the edge of the creek channel. If we spot crappie related to those baitfish, then we'll be sure that's a region we want to troll.

Question: Stokes, what electronics do you use, and how do you use them for your trolling with your Poles?

McClellan: We use a Lowrance depth finder with a built-in GPS. When we find the baitfish, we pay close attention to the depth where the baitfish are holding. If we see crappie related to those schools of bait, we also note at what depth the crappie are holding.

Once we have this information, we search for places where we can troll for at least 1/4-mile without having to turn around or pick up our poles and move. Ideally, we like to be able to troll for 1 to 1-1/2-miles before we have to relocate. So, we collect all this information and lay out a game plan before the tournament begins.

Question: Stokes, how do you decide what color jig to use once you have all this information?

McClellan: We start immediately breaking down the color we'll be fishing based on the water clarity and the weather conditions, and whether the area around the lake has a clear or a cloudy sky, because both these factors affect light penetration. We know that in a clear lake on a bright, sunny day, we'll probably need lighter-colored jigs. But if the water's dingy or muddy, or the day's overcast, we know we'll probably have to use darker-colored jigs. After we've determined at what depth the crappie are holding, we'll use our Color-C-Lector to dictate the jig color we'll start trolling with, because the crappie have to see the jigs, if they're going to take them. If they don't see the jigs, they won't bite them.

If we spot the crappie holding at 12 feet, we'll drop the Color-C-Lector down to 10 feet, because we want our jigs to run about 2 feet above the crappie. Since crappie look up for their baits, they may never see your jigs if they run below them. The Color-C-Lector gives us a primary color and a secondary color. The primary color is usually the darker part of the color the crappie can see, and the secondary color usually will be a fluorescent color. Once we know the primary and the secondary colors, we may choose to troll other jigs with those shades of colors on our poles. For black, we may run some deep-blue colors, and for chartreuse, we may try light chartreuse and dark chartreuse.

Using Scientific Reconnaissance

You can develop a game plan on how to fish for crappie at a new lake. This information will bring a large number of potential crappie hot spots to mind. Also, depending on the time of year you plan to fish, you must consider where the crappie will be along their seasonal migration routes.

You need to learn all you can about crappie and their migration routes because during the hot summer months or the cold winter months, you'll find crappie on deep-water structures, like underwater points, creek channels, ledges, humps and bridge pilings you've located from your map and aerial reconnaissance. When fishing the prespawn or the postspawn, search for crappie in staging areas, including the brush in front of piers, around marinas and boat docks and on humps, creek channels close to spawning flats and edges of creek channels in flooded-timber regions. If you fish the spawn, fish those hidden areas where other anglers won't fish. Cross the sandbars and the mud flats to reach the backs of bays and creeks cut off from the main river channel. When fishing relatively clear water during the spawn, concentrate on the humps and the points out in the lake. Many times crappie will spawn in deeper water, if the water's clear.

The state fisheries' biologist responsible for the lake you plan to fish provides one of the best places to gain information about a new lake. Obtain this biologist's name by calling your state fish and wildlife service. When you talk with the fisheries biologist, tell him where you want to fish. Ask him to suggest areas where his lake surveys indicate fishermen have caught the most crappie. Also question him about specific fishing sites, the depth of the water the crappie usually hold in at the time of year you want to fish and the kind of structure where the fish will hold. Too, inquire about parts of the lake where he's seen crappie during his electrofishing surveys, although most anglers may not fish these areas.

Your state fisheries biologist studies the lakes in his district throughout the year to try and determine the size, the number and the growth rate of the crappie as well as the water conditions. He has a vast amount of information that can help you learn how to fish a new lake.

Utilizing Old Maps for Secret Crappie Hot Spots Year-Round

One of the best ways to find crappie all year is to obtain an old map of the impounded property before the lake was filled. From these old maps, you can identify old home sites, road beds, lakes, stone walls, creek channels and a wide variety of structures that may not be marked on modern-day maps. These different types of structures offer some relief off the bottom where crappie can concentrate. Most serious crappie fishermen will build a stake bed or a brush shelter on the edges of creek or river channels to hold crappie. But if you can locate an old road bed, either automobile or railroad, and build brush shelters on the tops, the sides and at the bottoms of them, you can create productive crappie hot spots that often will pay off all year for you.

Anglers on Lake Eufaula in east Alabama on the Alabama/Georgia border often catch their limits of crappie at any time of the year by fishing old underwater bridges by day and night. When Lake Eufaula was inundated, the bridges weren't destroyed. These fishermen like to fish over an underwater bridge because a bridge will hold crappie throughout the year. They use grappling hooks to hold onto the bridge at the front and the back of the boat with bungee cords coming from the grappling hook to the tie-down rope. The bungee cords allow the boat to rock back and forth with the waves, yet still hold the boat directly over the bridge. The anglers put out lanterns on one side of the boat and let their lines down so that the lines run right down the edge of the bridge to hold the minnows just below the bridge. Then the crappie under the bridge can see the minnows. During the first hour after dark, these anglers catch most of the crappie holding under the bridge. However, as they continue to fish, the crappie seem to come out from under the bridge, hold on top of the bridge and then finally move right up under the lights.

Many reservoirs have submerged bridges in them. You'll find this technique deadly effective during July to catch big slabs by starlight. Although most people consider Lake Eufaula primarily a big-bass lake, the lake also homes numbers of 3/4- to 1-1/2-pound crappie. You can catch crappie when the weather sizzles, if you know where the fish hold, what triggers them to bite, and what baits to use for the most success.

Too, when the weather heats-up, you can fish small streams and tributaries off main lakes to find and catch big crappie. Many of these small creeks are spring-fed and often will run over small rapids and tiny waterfalls, which help oxygenate the water. By using a portable depth finder with your canoe, flat-bottom johnboat or one- or two-man boats, you often can locate underwater drop-offs or ledges in these small streams. When the water temperature in the stream is cooler than the water temperature in the main lake, as it often is in the summer months, the crappie will hold in the small creeks and streams in these holes, drop-offs, ledges and brush piles.

Oftentimes the big console-mounted depth finder/GPS are great devices to use on big waters. But when you're fishing a small stream, a portable depth finder and a small hand-held GPS receiver can be just as effective for pinpointing stream crappie. When you're fishing small streams, you may find shorter poles to be much-more effective than the longer poles.

Making Stake Beds

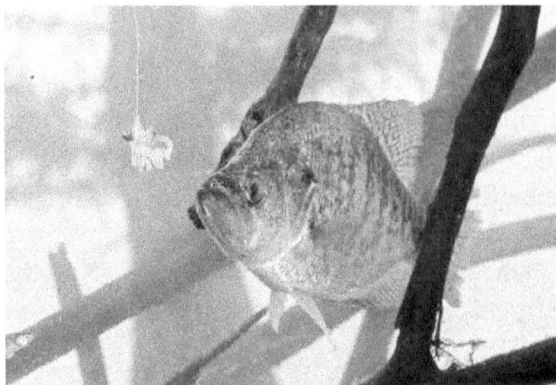

Editor's Note: Mike Biggs of Greenville, Tennessee, makes and puts-out new fish attractors in a very-short time every time he goes crappie fishing.

I've learned that by using a GPS receiver to locate my fish attractors and by putting-out plenty of fish attractors every time I go fishing, I can catch crappie almost any day I'm on the water. For many years, I've tried to put-out brush and stake beds. I have one of those power drivers that will drive the stakes into the bottom of a lake or a river. But those power drivers will work you to death. I've found a much-easier way to create crappie habitat and build new crappie hot spots every time I go fishing.

I start with a 5-gallon bucket, put wooden stakes in the bucket and pour concrete into the bucket. Once the concrete sets-up, it holds the wooden stakes in place and also is heavy enough to keep the 5-gallon bucket and wood on the bottom where I've placed it. I can build these 5-gallon stake buckets in my backyard during the week. When I get ready to go fishing, I carry 5- to 10-stake buckets with me. On the way to my fishing spot, I can place them in the areas where I want them. I'll usually put five buckets in a line about 100-feet apart on the edges of 8- to 16-foot drop-offs or ledges. I mark each one of these reefs as a waypoint on my GPS receiver. When I return to fish these spots, I can put my trolling motor down and quickly and efficiently move from one bucket reef to the next.

Therefore, instead of fishing a reef and running 4 miles down the lake to find another place to fish, I will fish five to 10 different artificial reefs by simply using my trolling motor and moving from one reef to the next. Since crappie move around a lot, they are not always in the same depth of water or on the same line of reefs. By having various lines of reefs in different water depths in separate areas of the lake, I always have some type of structure to fish where I can catch crappie.

I'm fishing these reefs with my B 'n' M Poles. I like the 10- and the 11-foot poles with the cork handles. I use 8-pound-test main line, put an egg-shaped slip sinker up the line and tie a snap swivel onto the end of the line. Before I go fishing, I'll tie up to 20 to 40, 1/16-ounce jigs each, on 18-inch 6-pound test leader with a loop on the end of the leader. This way, if I get hung, I can simply break the jig off on the 6-pound-test line, reel up my weight and swivel, unsnap the swivel, remove the old leader and quickly attach a new leader with a loop on the end of the line that has a jig on the other end of the leader. This is the quickest way I know to re-rig jigs and get right back to fishing.

Chapter 12 - What Other Tips Will Help You Catch Crappie

When to Set the Hook on Crappie with Sam Heaton

Editor's Note: Sam Heaton, Jr. of Port Saint Lucie, Florida, once guided crappie fishermen on Weiss Lake on the Alabama/Georgia border, about 200 days a year. He earned his living knowing when to set the hook on crappie and helped design crappie poles. Today Heaton splits his time between fishing for saltwater and freshwater fish. He particularly enjoys fishing for crappie at Florida's Lake Okeechobee, Lake Istokpoga and Lake Garcia.

"When the fish takes the bait and the cork goes down fast, I wait until I lose sight of the cork before I strike the fish," Heaton says. "I want the fish to get the hook deep enough in its mouth and not in the lips. If the crappie is a good-sized fish, I don't want to lose it by trying to pull the crappie through the brush and having the hook tear out. The trick to setting the hook properly is to put enough weight on your line to make your cork sit halfway down in the water. Then it's much-more sensitive to a strike when it's floating higher in the water. You also can detect a strike more quickly and easily. If I see my cork, which has been halfway down in the water, floating sideways on top of the water, I strike the fish immediately. I know a crappie has taken the bait deep enough in its mouth as it swims toward the surface for me to get a good hook set."

Another hook-setting problem we've all encountered when fishing with a cork and a jig is when to set the hook if we're casting to the bank and retrieving the cork and jig to us. According to Heaton, "When I'm fishing a hollow, heart-shaped, tapered bobber, I drill a small hole in the bobber. I put three pieces of BB-sized lead in the bobber to give it some weight, which makes the bobber and the jig much easier to cast. Also the bobber is much-more sensitive to a strike because it sits much deeper in the water than usual – about halfway down. Then I seal the hole with silicone. As I start a slow, steady retrieve, I set the hook immediately if I feel or see a strike. Although I fool that fish into believing the jig is a live bait, the crappie won't stay fooled long. Once the fish feels that hard, lead jig, it'll spit the jig out if you don't set the hook quickly."

Yet another hook-setting situation that's difficult for most anglers is when they're fishing a deep drop-off for suspended crappie, using light line and little jigs and trying to catch the fish as the bait falls. "When I'm fishing a small jig and light line in deep water, I usually see 75 percent of my strikes on the line before I ever feel them," Heaton comments. "To be able to spot the strike, I use a highly-visible line. When I see the line twitching, moving or jumping as the bait's falling, I set the hook. If the bait falls all the way to the bottom and I don't get a strike, I'll jerk the bait up off the bottom quickly to jump it 3 or 4 feet across the bottom. Then I watch the line for a strike as the jig falls back to the bottom. I'll strike the fish as soon as I see the line move, because I believe a crappie is more likely to spit out the artificial bait than it is a live minnow. To give myself more time to strike the fish, I usually put scent on my lures to help the fish hold the bait in its mouth a fraction longer and give me the time I need to set the hook and catch the fish."

In a scenario where Heaton is fishing a tight line with a jig in 8 to 12 feet of water in a stump field, he recommends you know the water depth through which your jig is passing to have a successful hook set. "If I'm fishing in 15 feet of water with a 1/24-ounce jig on 6-pound-test line, I assume the jig will fall at the rate of one foot per second. I count the jig down to about 10 feet and then start a slow, steady retrieve back to the boat. If I don't get a strike, I'll let the jig fall to 11 feet and repeat the process. When the jig's down to 14 feet, and I get a strike, I assume my jig's still passing above the stumps. After you've been fishing for awhile, you'll be able to feel the difference between a solid stump and a crappie strike."

I next asked Heaton when and how he sets the hook when trolling jigs or minnows. "I let the boat set the hook when I'm trolling for crappie," Heaton explains. "If I have a fish on the line, I sweep the rod or the pole forward when I see the fish on, but I'm not really setting the hook. All I'm trying to do is get the fish's head turned toward the boat to make the crappie easier to reel. Remember, you're not attempting to catch a marlin, a tarpon or an amberjack with hard, bony mouths. You're trying to take a papermouth. The boat delivers enough force to hook for a good hook set. Don't add any force to your strike, or you'll tear the hook out of the crappie's mouth."

How to Fish on the Rocks

Editor's Note: Rick Solomon of Piqua, Ohio, and his partner, Mike Walters, have been crappie-fishing together for more than 20 years and fish tournaments.

Question: Why do y'all fish on the rocks, and what are the rocks?

Solomon: Rocks are the riprap you find along the edge of bridges and highways, or the type of rocks along lake home fronts or on rocky banks. We fish this way mostly in the North when the shad start moving onto the rocks to feed on algae. When the water warms-up, and the rocks begin to develop algae, the shad will move onto the rocks to feed on the algae. The crappie will follow the shad into the rocks. We've even caught black crappie creating beds and bedding on the rocks in some lakes. We've found this happening on Lake Shelbyville in Illinois, Coralville Lake in Iowa, Grand Lake St. Marys in Ohio and other lakes in the North that have riprap.

Question: How close to the rocks are you finding the fish?

Solomon: We've caught crappie in 6 to 8 inches of water right up against the rocks. We've seen the crappie chase the shad into the rocks. We usually troll the rocks. Our first pole will be up against the shoreline, trolling our baits in 6 to 8 inches of water; the second pole will be a little bit further out from the riprap, trolling our baits in 12 to 14 inches of water; and our third pole may be 1-1/2-feet deep, trolling along the edge of the riprap

Question: You mentioned that you've seen black crappie bedding in the rocks. Is that right?

150

Solomon: Yes; in certain lakes, at specific times of the year, we've caught black crappie bedding in the rocks.

Question: What's the key to knowing which rocks to fish and which rocks not to fish for crappie?

Solomon: We've found that the only rocks that produce crappie for us are riprap in protected areas. The rocks need to be off the main river channel and out of the wind, especially a north wind.

Question: How did you first find crappie on the rocks?

Walters: We were fishing in Coralville in Iowa, and we saw anglers sitting on the riprap, casting out and catching crappie. We wanted to find a more-productive way to catch more fish. When you see anglers sitting on riprap catching crappie, you don't have to be a rocket scientist to understand that there's crappie on those rocks. The next question you have to answer is, how you catch the most and the biggest crappie in the shortest time? For us, that means trolling with poles along the rocks. Crappie fishing is a numbers game. The more crappie you catch, the better your odds are for catching big crappie. We've found that by trolling the rocks with our poles, we can catch numbers of crappie quickly and throw the crappie back that aren't really big. We're trying to weigh-in the seven biggest crappie we can catch. In many areas of the country, you'll see bank-bound anglers fishing off jetties and riprap. If those anglers are catching crappie, then you can catch more crappie, if you troll the same areas they're fishing and stay out of the way. If you fish from the bank, you still can catch the crappie that are moving in to spawn on the riprap. We use 12- to 16-foot poles when we're trolling rocks, but we'll run the tip of our rod within 2 feet of the shoreline.

151

Question: Do you put poles out on the other side of the boat away from the rocks when you're trolling this way?

Walters: Typically, we do, depending on what state we're fishing in and how many poles we're able to fish at one time. We usually fish anywhere from four to six poles, depending on where we're fishing. However, we've found that if the crappie are really moving into the rocks, the poles on the other side of the boat are pretty-much useless. The crappie are forcing the shad into the rocks where they can feed on them. They're not holding off the rocks, waiting to move-in and spawn.

Question: How long will the crappie usually hold on the rocks?

Walters: We've found that in the North, this is usually a summer pattern. This pattern can start in the late spring and last through the summer. We haven't experimented with it very much in the fall. However, I did catch some crappie at Salt Fork Lake in Ohio in October. But on this day, the crappie were further away from the rocks, and the poles on the outside of the boat were producing almost as well as the poles on the inside of the boat, next to the rocks. However, we've found that in late spring, usually the two poles that are closest to the rocks on the shoreline produce the most crappie. Although we said that you need to fish protected areas, wave action is a positive factor for catching crappie on the rocks. We've noticed that when there's a little bit of wave action, and the shad get bounced-up against the rocks and become injured, these injured shad make an easy meal for the crappie. Remember that the rocks are primarily a feeding area for the crappie.

Question: Mike, you said that you and Rick have found this tactic to be the most productive in the North. Do you think it will work in the South?

Walters: I believe that anytime you see shad feeding along the edge of riprap, or you spot anglers fishing from the riprap and catching crappie, you can assume this tactic will work, regardless of where you're fishing in the country.

Question: Do you think that the reasons the crappie are coming to the rocks when the sun hits the rocks, the rocks give off more heat and have warmer water closer to them than other structure in the lake, or, do you believe that the crappie aren't seeking the warm water as much as they're looking for the shad feeding on the algae at the rocks?

Walters: The crappie are on the rocks to eat the shad that's feeding on the algae. For the rocks to be effective, you must have a plankton bloom in the algae growth to pull the shad to the rocks. When the shad come in to the riprap, the crappie and the bass have to follow them, because the shad are their primary food source.

Question: What kinds of rocks are the most productive?

Walters: We've found that the big boulder type of rocks are the most-effective rocks to find crappie.

Question: Where else have you found crappie?

Walters: Besides quickly trolling the rocks, we've found that the crappie will often hold right behind big rocks that break the current and any rocks that stick out into the water further than other rocks do. You'll find crappie holding on any irregular features along the shoreline. The furthest we've ever caught crappie away from the rocks when they're in this riprap is probably 6-feet away from the shoreline. This is strictly a shoreline tactic. We've also found that wherever the rocks stop, we don't find any more crappie. We haven't caught any crappie in the transition area where the rocks stop and the bank begins.

How to Pinpoint and Fish Deep Brush for Crappie

Editor's Note: Competitive bass fishing is one of the best activities that can take place on a lake to help crappie fishermen. Tournament bass anglers will go to great lengths to ensure they can find and catch bass on places no one else knows. They'll sink brush on points and river ledges, in the center of bays, along river and creek channels and in areas where bass naturally travel and hold. This brush bass fishermen sink also makes ideal crappie hot spots. Because the crappie don't know the brush has been sunk solely for bass, they'll move into the brush and hold there just like bass will.

"Use your depth finder to survey main river and creek points and secondary points on lakes that have heavy bass-fishing pressure, and you'll find brush on just about every one of these points," Jackie Thompson, a bass-fishing and crappie-fishing guide on Lake Eufaula near Eufaula, Alabama, explains. "This brush usually will be sunk on the break line, and crappie will hold where they find the brush. These brush piles on points can provide productive crappie fishing during the prespawn and postspawn. The crappie will use the brush on the points as staging areas before they move into the creeks to spawn and also when hot weather runs the crappie out of the creeks and back towards the deep water."

If you find the brush shelters built, you can consistently take crappie throughout most of the year but especially during the spawn. Keeping the location of your brush shelter a secret is also a very-important key to finding more crappie in your brush each time you fish it. By locating deep-water brush shelters where most crappie fishermen don't fish, you increase your odds for having productive brush shelters to fish year-round.

Where to Sink Deep Brush

Sam Spencer of Montgomery, Alabama, formerly Alabama's Chief of the Fisheries Section of Alabama's Department of Conservation for two decades, has studied how and where to sink brush in lake to act as effective crappie attractors because his family likes to catch and eat crappie. "The first thing I learned was that hardwoods like oak, hickory and poplar seemed to attract more crappie than pine, cedar and other evergreens," Spencer reports. "I didn't really understand why these hardwood trees seemed to be preferred by crappie, but I knew I consistently caught more crappie off the hardwoods than the evergreens."

Once Spencer determined what type of brush he should be sinking to catch crappie, he started to study what kinds of areas he should sink his brush in to produce the most crappie at any time of the year. "I've learned that the brush shelters, sunk in coves with little or no other brush in them, consistently produce the most fish prior to, during and after the spawn," Spencer mentions. "Apparently the less cover a crappie has to select from, the more fish your brush shelters will attract."

Another factor that makes deep-water brush shelters in the centers of coves very productive is because crappie often move in to the center of a cove prior to the spawn and hold in the deep water there before the spawn, waiting on the water temperature and the photoperiod to become right and trigger the spawn. Even if the brush shelter is in no more than 8 to 10 feet of water in the center of a cove prior to the spawn, the crappie will move into this brush as the weather warms up and hold there. After the crappie spawn, they'll generally return to this deep-water brush before going back to their summer, deep-water homes. "As the time for the spawn draws near, most crappie fishermen are looking for papermouths on the bank," Spencer says. "Very-few anglers will be looking for or fishing deep-water brush in the center of a cove. Therefore, brush piles placed at these locations rarely will be found or fished but will pay crappie dividends."

Another favorite site of Spencer's to place brush shelters in the deep water is along rocky banks and sheer rock bluffs. " Most crappie fishermen seldom look for crappie in these spots. Since these areas usually are devoid of any type of cover, you can concentrate crappie in them." Generally, Spencer waits two or three days before he returns to fish these brush shelters once he sinks them. "But I have sunk a brush shelter in the morning, gone back to it in the afternoon and caught 50 crappie from that spot."

How to Find Natural Deep-Water Brush Structures

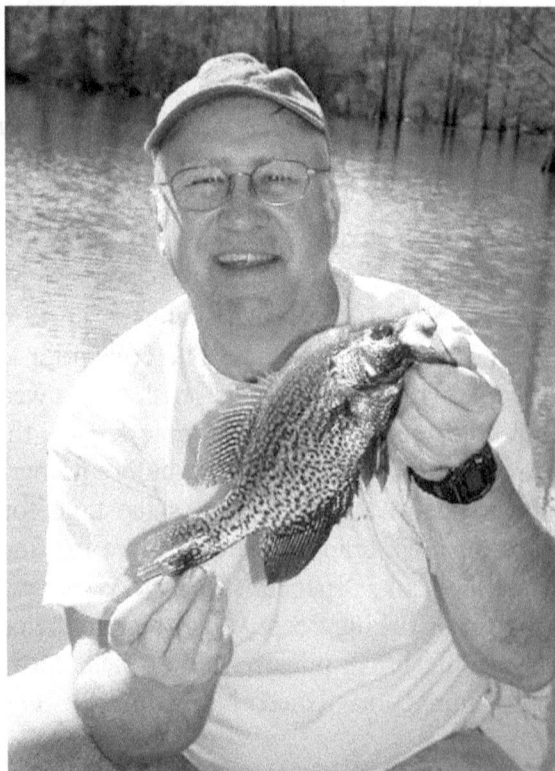

While the weather was still cold and before most anglers even thought about crappie fishing each year, the late Curt Edney of Midfield, Alabama, would bring-in limits of prespawn crappie. No one ever really understood where Edney was fishing or how he was able to take so many big crappie. But one day almost 25-years ago, he shared his secret. "I know where there are hundreds of big trees under the water no one ever fishes," Edney said. "The less fishing pressure a site gets, the more big crappie you're likely to

158

catch – especially if those hot spots are well away from the bank and no one can see them."

Edney, who fished in the days before the depth finder was used in fresh water, had developed a unique strategy for finding deep-water brush piles. "I look at the bank and try to locate old stumps or holes in the bank where a tree once has stood that's been blown into the lake by high winds, " Edney explained. "At most of these spots, the trunks of the trees in the water may be rotted away. However, often the limbs in the top of the tree still will be preserved under the water. To locate the top, I look at a live tree on the bank near where I see the fallen tree's stump or stump hole and guess where the top of the nearby live tree will land if that tree falls. Then I put my boat in about the spot where I think the top should be and begin to cast a 1/4-once jig. I'm not really trying to catch crappie; I'm just hoping I'll get hung on some tree limbs.

"I swim my jig close to the bottom. Once the jig gets hung, I move my boat until I'm straight over the spot where my jig has hung. I carefully ease a marker buoy over the side of the boat. Then I break off my jig and re-rig with a 1/16 – or a 1/24-ounce crappie jig. I bend the hook on the jig to make it directly in line with the lead head of the jig. Then the head of the jig acts as a bumper to keep the point of the hook from being hung in the brush as I try to pinpoint the limbs and brush under the water. Most of the time, I'll find and catch crappie out in the middles of the creeks and bays where other people never fish. Once I'm through fishing an area, I look for a landmark on the bank, note the spot in my logbook, pull up my buoy and leave the region." The next time Edney returned to this site, he didn't use a marker buoy to find the deep-water tree top. He just knew where it was and fished it. Today anglers can use their GPS receivers to locate the waypoints where they've found brush.

How to Fish Brush at Boathouses and Docks

Many lakeside residents put brush shelters out for crappie under their piers and docks. Some property owners also sink brush in front of the docks. If a dock has pole holders on it, more than likely the brush won't be more than 10 to 20 yards in front of the dock. If the dock has chairs, seats or benches on it, the brush usually will be within 30 yards (casting distance) of the dock. Just like bass fishermen flip docks with a pig and jig to catch bass, crappie fisherman fish out in the front of docks to take big crappie. You often can locate brush in 10 to 20 feet of water. Since deep-water brush generally holds crappie year-round, by finding and fishing 10 to 30 docks in a day, often a crappie fisherman can limit out on deep-water crappie prior to the spawn by just fishing docks. This dock-fishing pattern generally produces best during the middle of the week when few lake residents are at home and not many other fishermen are on the lake.

How and Why to Sink Brush on River and Creek Ledges

The most-consistent place to find crappie at any time of the year is often along the edges of the underwater creekbanks and riverbanks. These banks usually have stumps on them. Water will wash the dirt away form the roots of the stumps, which then provide ambush spots where crappie can and will hold. However, if you are fishing in an area with a large number of stumps along the edge an old creek or river channel, many times if you put brush on the edge of that creek channel, you can concentrate more crappie around the brush than around the stumps. The more cover the crappie have to hold on, the more crappie you can concentrate on that cover.

One of the best places to sink brush on the edge of a creek channel is near a bridge piling on the down-current side. Most crappie fishermen will fish around bridge pilings on the edge of creek and river channels because they know crappie will use the bridge pilings as spots to hold when moving up the creeks to spawn and swimming out of the creeks after the spawn. Bridge pilings are easy to find and fish. However, if you'll move 10- to 20-yards downstream of the bridge piling and build a brush shelter on the edge of the creek channel, you can have a deep-water crappie hot spot that probably will produce plenty of crappie and receive very little fishing pressure. For this type of fishing structure to be productive, sink the brush close enough to the bridge piling so the piling will break the current, and the brush won't be swept away. But put the brush far enough away from the piling that the crappie fishermen who normally fish the piling won't be able to find it. This type of deep-water brush shelter on the edge of a creek channel can and will short-stop the crappie that normally hold on the bridge piling and give you a productive deep-water hotspot where you can find and take crappie before and after the spawn.

Chapter 13 - Why to Bulldoze Crappie

Editor's Note: Avid crappie fisherman and tournament angler Ronnie Capps, of Tiptonville, Tennessee, has developed with his partner a crappie technique they call bulldozing.

Question: What's bulldozing?

Capps: My partner Steve Coleman and I have been using a tactic we call bulldozing for quite a few years. Just like a bulldozer tries to push over a tree, a rock or a stump, we use our Minn Kota trolling motor to try and push against the brush in deep water with our Capps and Coleman Minnow Rigs.

Question: Ronnie, explain bulldozing.

Capps: Steve and I sit on the front of the boat with two rods each in our rod holders. We use a 3/4-ounce sinker on each Capps and Coleman Minnow Rig and our trolling motor to mash those Minnow Rigs right into deep-water brush.

Question: How do you mash those minnow rigs into the brush?

Capps: I cast a marker buoy upcurrent of the brush or a treetop that we'll be bulldozing. Then I motor my boat downcurrent below the buoy and put out my B'n'M crappie pole. We approach the brush either from downwind or downcurrent, depending on which is the strongest. We let our Capps and Coleman Minnow Rigs down to the right depth and then start moving the boat toward the brush pile. When I see one of my poles start to bend as it's pushing my Minnow Rig into the brush, I reduce the power I'm giving the trolling motor. Then all the Minnow Rigs on the four poles are mashed into the brush. To consistently catch crappie using this tactic, let the Minnow Rigs get hung-up in the brush, and don't try to keep them from getting hung. Once we know we've got our leads and minnow rigs in the brush, we try to keep our boat pointed right at the brush, use a little bit of force from the trolling motor to keep our lines pushing against the brush and then wait on a crappie bite. The minnows down below are zigging to the left and the right because they're in the brush and probably looking at a crappie. We've found that the crappie have to bite when you mash those minnows right in front of their faces.

Question: Okay, Ronnie, when you get on a crappie, how do you land it, because your lines are either hung-up or about to be hung-up in the brush?

Capps: When I feel the bite, I set the hook and pull the crappie either to the right or the left of the boat. I slowly reduce the power on the trolling motor, so the boat drifts away from the brush. Since the boat is moving away from the brush, I often can pull the crappie out of the brush. As soon as I hit the brush, I'll either reduce the power to the trolling motor or use my trolling motor to push me back away from the brush. Then I can pull the crappie out of the brush and into the boat. Most of the time when we start backing away from the brush, we can pull the crappie out of the brush because we're pulling it to us the same way we approach the brush. For this technique to be successful, use 15-pound-test fluorocarbon P Line. I prefer the heavier line because the wire hooks on the Capps and Coleman Minnow Rigs will straighten-out as we back- out of the brush. Then, when we get our Minnow Rigs in to our boat, we can bend our hooks back to their original shapes. Ronnie and I have learned that if you don't get hung-up, you won't catch crappie. We've found that using heavy 15-pound-test line and having our hooks bend straight as we pull them out of the brush, instead of using lighter line, breaking off our Minnow Rigs and then having to re-rig every time we go into the brush with our bait, is far more efficient.

Question: Ronnie, walk me up your double-minnow rig.

Capps: At the very end of the minnow rig, there's a No. 214-2 Eagle Claw light-wire bronze hook, which is attached to 12-pound-test leader about 12-inches long. The leader's attached to the main line with about a 3/4-ounce sinker on it. Then the line runs from the sinker up about 30 inches to a Hi-Tech Tackle three-way in-line swivel. Coming off one of the eyes of the three-way swivel will be an 11-inch drop line with another No. 214-2 Eagle Claw light-wire bronze hook. On the third eye of the swivel, we tie our main line, which is 15-pound-test fluorocarbon P-Line. Many anglers fish a smaller main line than I do, like 6- to 8-pound-test line. But these anglers break-off more minnow rigs than I do. I've learned over the years that I'd rather be fishing with heavy line than re-tying minnow rigs on every time I go to a brush pile.

Question: What pole do you use when you're bulldozing?

Capps: I prefer the B'n'M 14-foot Capps & Coleman Series Trolling rods.

Question: What reel do you use on these poles?

Capps: I fish with the spinning reels designed to be used with these poles. We only put about 60 feet of line on these reels, because we won't be using them for casting. We've found that 60 feet is about all the line we need when we're using our bulldozing tactic.

Question: Ronnie, most people aren't fishing in water that deep, are they?

Capps: No, they're not. Most crappie fishermen remember that they've caught crappie in 2 to 6 feet of water during the spring spawn. But in the summer, the crappie return to the same spots where they've been holding during the winter months, which will be on that deep structure. As the water clears-up, you've got to fish deeper. We actually catch some male crappie colored-up like they are during the spawn in 20 feet of water. In most of these really-clear lakes, the crappie spawn much deeper than most people think.

A Conversation with Author John E. Phillips

Question: John, a lot of the information in this book you've gathered from tournament crappie fishermen. Why?

Phillips: That's a very-good question, and the answer's simple. The tournament crappie fishermen have to catch the most big crappie they can every day they compete, if they're going to earn any money to continue to pay their expenses, be able to go to crappie tournaments and be able to add some cash to their family's income. They're highly motivated to find the most big crappie they can in the short time they have to fish in a tournament – often no more than 1 or 2 days.

Question: How long have you been crappie fishing?

Phillips: I was fortunate to have a dad who worked and lived through the Great Depression. He and my mother were what's known as "close providers." Growing up, we were just above the poverty level, but we never knew it. The main reason for the hunting and fishing that we did was not only for sport and fellowship, but to feed our family. In those days, even when we caught small fish, we scored them across the sides, fried them whole and pulled the meat away from the bone. I always liked catching crappie, but I liked eating crappie even more. When my wife and I were at the University of West Alabama, I had a friend named John Holley, one of the best crappie fishermen I'd ever known. He and I would fish together on either Friday or Saturday. We caught all the crappie we legally could catch and had a fish fry for the other students living in the married students' apartments. During the week, I'd crappie-fish in a creek that was only 5-minutes from campus before or after school and work and catch crappie from the bank to eat in the middle of the week. I guess the best way to explain how long I've been crappie fishing is to say I never remember a time when I haven't fished for crappie.

Question: John, many of the techniques that the pros talk about in this book involve trolling or drift-fishing with multiple poles, often in open water or even using crankbaits. Why do you not talk very much about fishing with a single pole and live bait?

Phillips: For most of my life, I've fished with a single pole and live minnows. However, this is not the most-efficient way to find and catch the most big crappie in the shortest time. For me, hand-poling with live bait is one of my favorite ways to fish, because it's relaxing and exciting all at the same time. This technique is one I've used throughout my crappie-fishing career, until professional crappie fishing changed the world of fishing for speckled-sides, just like professional bass fishing changed forever the sport of bass fishing. Because pro fishermen have to find and catch more and bigger fish more quickly, most of the new innovations in tackle and the new techniques have come from this new group of anglers. Unlike in the old days, when you never told anyone where you were fishing or how you were fishing, these professional crappie fishermen will share their knowledge and their strategies to help me and you find and take more crappie.

Question: What do you think are some of the most-revolutionary changes in the way we fish for crappie?

Phillips: I think the number-one change that's made the most impact is side-scanning depth finders that enable you to exactly mark the spot where you find the crappie with a GPS waypoint, either under your boat or to the left or right side of your boat. This new depth finder not only allows you to see the fish and/or the structures, but by being able to mark the spots as waypoints, even if your boat doesn't pass right over them, you can find locations to fish faster and easier than ever. You can spend 2 or 3 hours in the morning finding schools of crappie with your depth finder and then return to these schools throughout the day and try to catch the fish. Two-other big changes are the growths of spider rigging (multiple-pole trolling) and using crankbaits to troll for open-water crappie.

Author's Page

I have spent all my life hunting for great people and fishing for great stories. My journey through the writer's life has been a continuing-education program to learn all I can every day and pass along what I've learned through the written word. My journey has been full of excitement, enjoyment and discovery, and I hope you'll find much of what I've found in the words of my books.

John E. Phillips, the 2008 Crossbow Communicator of the year and the 2007 Legendary Communicator chosen for induction into the National Fresh Water Hall of Fame, is a freelance writer (over 6,000 magazine articles for about 100 magazines and several thousand newspaper columns published), magazine editor, photographer for print media as well as industry catalogues (over 25,000 photos published), lecturer, outdoor consultant, marketing consultant, book author and daily internet content provider with an overview of the outdoors. Phillips has been a contributor to many national magazines, has been affiliated with 27-radio stations across Alabama serving as their outdoor editor and wrote for a weekly syndicated column, "Alabama Outdoors," for 38-Alabama newspapers for more than 13 years. Phillips was Outdoor Editor for the "Birmingham

Post-Herald" for 24 years. Phillips was also the executive editor for "Great Days Outdoors" magazine for 3 years.

The author of almost 30 books on the outdoors, Phillips is a founding member of the Professional Outdoor Media Association (POMA) and an active member of the Southeastern Outdoors Press Association (SEOPA). Phillips also is the owner of Night Hawk Publications, a marketing and publishing firm, and president of Creative Concepts, an outdoor consulting group.

Phillips conducts seminars across the nation at colleges in freelance writing, photography and outdoor education besides teaching courses in how to sell what you write to writers' groups. Phillips received his photography training as a still-lab photo specialist for six years in the Air Force. He was the chief photographer for Mannequins, Inc., a Birmingham modeling agency, for 11 years.

While serving as 2nd Vice President of the Alabama Wildlife Federation, Phillips was in charge of all press releases for the organization as well as serving as Chairman of Alabama's Big Buck Contest, which he founded more than 35-years ago. He also was president of the Alabama Sportsman's Association for 3 years.

Phillips is the recipient of a Certificate of Merit from the Governor of Alabama and the Department of Conservation for his work in the outdoor field. Phillips is vitally interested in the outdoors and travels the nation collecting personalities, stories and how-to information for his articles and features.

EDUCATION: B.S. degree from the University of West Alabama with a physical education major and a history minor.

EXPERIENCE: 10 years part-time and fulltime physical director for YMCAs and 38 years as a freelance writer, photographer, editor, book author, lecturer and daily-content provider for websites. Currently, Phillips writes for magazines – both print and digital - and is a regular contributor to 12-internet magazines and a daily-content provider for 8 websites, besides the author of 1/2-dozen Kindle books, with more to come.

WRITING AWARDS: Runnerup - Best Outdoor Magazine Feature - 1981 - SEOPA; Certificate of Merit - Awarded by Alabama's Governor for writings on conservation; Most Outstanding Sports Writer in Southeast - 1983 & 1984; Best Outdoor Feature in Alabama, 1987 - Alabama Sportswriters' Association 3rd Place; Best Book of the Year - 1989 - SEOPA; 2007 - inducted into the National Fresh Water Fishing Hall of Fame as a Legendary Communicator; 2008 - received award naming him 2008 Crossbow Communicator of the Year from the Crossbow Manufacturers' Association; 2009 - GAMMA Honorable Mention for Consumer/Paid Best Essay for July/August 2008 in "Southern Sporting Journal;" 2012 – chosen as a contributor to "The Best of the Writer Magazine."

More Fishing and Hunting Books by John E. Phillips

Go to www.amazon.com/kindle, type John E. Phillips into Search and click on Author's Page (2nd choice) when it comes up to see books available, or go to www.nighthawkpublications.com, and on the left-hand side of the page, click on eBooks to learn more.

The 10 Sins of Turkey Hunting with Preston Pittman

13 Breakfast Recipes You Can't Live Without

13 Chili Recipes You Can't Live Without

13 Deer Recipes You Can't Live Without

13 Freshwater Fish Recipes You Can't Live Without

13 Saltwater Fish Recipes You Can't Live Without

13 Seafood Recipes You Can't Live Without

13 Soup, Chowder and Gumbo Recipes You Can't Live Without

13 Stew Recipes You Can't Live Without

13 Wild Turkey Recipes You Can't Live Without

Alabama's Inshore Saltwater Fishing: A Year-Round Guide for Catching More Than 15 Species

Alabama's Offshore Saltwater Fishing: A Year-Round Guide for Catching Over 15 Species of Fish

America's Greatest Bass Fisherman

The Best Wild Game & Seafood Cookbook Ever: 350 Southern Recipes for Deer, Turkey, Fish, Seafood, Small Game and Birds

Bowhunting Deer: The Secrets of the PSE Pros

Bowhunting the Dangerous Bears of Alaska

Catching Speckled Trout and Redfish: Learn from Alabama's Best Fishermen

Catch the Most and Biggest Bass in Any Lake: 18 Pro Fishermen's Best Tactics

Catfish Like a Pro

Courage: Stories of Hometown Heroes

Crappie: How to Catch them Spring and Summer

Deer & Fixings: How to Cook Delicious Venison

For Hot-Weather Fishing Success, Head to Reelfoot

Fishing Mississippi's Gulf Coast and Visitor's Guide

Hot-Weather Bass Tactics

How to Bass Fish Like a Pro

How to Become a Tournament Bass Fisherman

How to Find Your Elk and Get Him in Close

How to Fish Mississippi's Gulf Coast in June

How to Hunt Deer Like a Pro

How to Hunt Deer Up Close: With Bows, Rifles, Muzzleloaders and Crossbows

How to Hunt Turkeys with World Champion Preston Pittman

How to Make Money with Taxidermy: 70 Tips for Hunters and Small Businesses

How to Win a Bass Tournament: Personal Lessons from 8 Pro Bass Fishermen

Jim Crumley's Secrets of Bowhunting Deer

The John E. Phillips Sampler: Hunting, Fishing and More

The Most Dangerous Game with a Bow: Secrets of the PSE Pros

Moving Forward: Stories of Hometown Heroes

Outdoor Life's Complete Turkey Hunting

PhD Elk: How to Hunt the Smartest Elk in Any State

PhD Gobblers: How to Hunt the Smartest Turkeys in the World

PhD Whitetails: How to Hunt and Take the Smartest Deer on Any Property

The Recipes You Can't Live Without

The Recipes You Can't Live Without: Chilis, Stews, Soups, Chowders & Gumbo

The Recipes You Can't Live Without: Freshwater & Saltwater Fish & Seafood

Reelfoot Lake: How to Fish for Crappie, Bass, Bluegills and Catfish and Hunt for Ducks

Secrets for Catching Red Snapper and Grouper in the Gulf of Mexico

Secrets for Hunting Elk

The Turkey Hunter's Bible

Turkey Hunting Tactics

To buy my print books on hunting, visit: http://nighthawkpublications.com/hunting/hunting.htm. These books include:

"Black Powder Hunting Secrets"

"Complete Turkey Hunting"

"Deer & Fixings"

"How to Take Monster Bucks"

"Jim Crumley's Secrets of Bowhunting Deer"

"The Masters' Secrets of Bowhunting Deer"

"The Masters' Secrets of Deer Hunting"

"The Masters' Secrets of Turkey Hunting"

"PhD Gobblers"

"PhD Whitetails"

"The Science of Deer Hunting"

"Turkey Hunting Tactics"

For my fishing books, go to http://nighthawkpublications.com/fishing/fishing.htm. These books include:

"Bass Fishing Central Alabama"

"Fish & Fixings"

"Masters' Secrets of Catfishing"

"Masters' Secrets of Crappie Fishing"

Go to www.amazon.com and type in the names of our other print books to view them:

- The Turkey Hunter's Bible

- Crappie: How to Catch Them Spring and Summer

If you enjoyed this book, let us know by leaving a review on Amazon!

www.ingramcontent.com/pod-product-compliance
Lightning Source LLC
Chambersburg PA
CBHW060925040426

42445CB00011B/793